LITTLE MIRACLES

A MEMOIR

By

One love ♡

GERALD HAUSMAN

Stay Thirsty Publishing is proud to present this memoir, but the stories, experiences, memories, names and words in this book are attributable solely to the author.

For permissions to reproduce selections from this book, write to info@staythirstymedia.com - Att: Permissions.

ISBN: 9781078119214

STAY THIRSTY PRESS

An Imprint of Stay Thirsty Publishing

A Division of

STAY THIRSTY MEDIA, INC.

staythirsty.com

Also by Gerald Hausman

(Published by Stay Thirsty Press)

Not Since Mark Twain
The Forbidden Ride*

*Co-authored with Loretta Hausman

"I've seen a lot of little miracles in the night. I'm a fishermon, I fish for a long while and in the night I see the sky move! Sometimes ya cyan see for yourself--- ya find tings jus done in front of yuh and it looks like miracles."

-- Countryman, Jamaican actor and fisherman,
(in conversation with author Timothy White)

Table of Contents

Starting Out

The Greatest Whistler in the World, Columbia School Berkeley Heights, New Jersey (1956)

I met Fred Lowry, "The Greatest Whistler in the World" when I was ten.

He probably was the greatest whistler because when you heard him you couldn't believe he was a two-legged man. He was a bird. But he could also whistle symphonies.

I gave him a little sample of my own whistling abilities and he said, "Take it on the road. I did, and the world is better for it."

My mom was also a whistler. She could whistle birds out of the woods and they would land on her index finger. She was that good. She was better than Fred Lowry, I thought, because her whistles actually spoke to birds. She could speak vireo, crow, mockingbird.

So I grew up, as you might suppose, bird whistling.

And I traveled all over the United States, Europe and the Caribbean telling stories about animals and making the same sounds they made whether whistling, barking, grunting or growling.

From my dad who was a gymnast, I learned how do animal movements, horse or buffalo, and I could jump off a stage and land like a panther.

My mom said it wasn't enough to tell stories, I also needed to write them. She taught me how to write so that people paid attention. I made the sounds of animals in my written stories. The animals breathed, or so I believed.

So I grew up a whistler and a writer.

I have never looked back in regret at anything.

I still whistle, tumble, write and carry on like a four-legged creature on a stage of my own imagination.

I still talk to animals.

I had a conversation with a grasshopper yesterday.

He said, "The world is going to be a better place. Keep whistling."

The Man Who Talked to Animals
Westminster, Maryland (1950)

There was a bad bulldog that lived down at the end of our street. Everybody was afraid of that dog. Some people went to the other side of the street to avoid him. Others didn't bother going down our street at all. The bulldog was always there, waiting in the yard for somebody to come by. I tried ignoring him when I walked past the fenced yard, but as soon as I got to the locked gate, the bulldog charged me, hit the fence, and roared like a lion. I was so scared I ran all the way home.

When I told my dad about it, all he said was, "He'll come around."

"What do you mean?" I said. "That dog only comes around to bite you."

My dad smiled. "Give him some time."

But after a whole year that bad bulldog was just as vicious as ever.

One day my dad and I were walking past the bulldog's yard, and the animal ran at us, growling and flinging spit in all directions.

Only this time, the gate was open.

My dad said, "Stand perfectly still. Leave the rest to me."

The bulldog came up, snarling like a chainsaw.

When the bulldog got within an inch of us, my dad leaned down low, and talked to the dog. My dad spoke in a soft voice, and said – "You're nothing but a bully, and you have *no* friends. You *wish* you had friends, but you don't. And the reason you don't is because you scare everyone off. You make them *not want to like you*. So you're all alone. A mean bad bulldog *with no friends*. You *should* be ashamed of yourself."

I was shivering while my dad was talking. I thought the bulldog was going to attack. But instead, the dog started whimpering. And when my dad sympathized with him, the bulldog rolled on his back like a puppy.

Later, heading home, my dad told me, "You've got to level with them. Tell them the truth."

I was still puzzled. "Is that how it works with animals?"

"Yes," he said, "and that's how it works with people, too."

"I wish I could be like that."

"You *can* – just remember to treat everyone the way you want to be treated, and if someone does something wrong, tell them about it. Look into their eyes, and tell them how you feel."

"Do animals understand *everything* we say?" I asked.

"If we *want* them to," he answered.

"What about insects?"

"Insects, too."

"What about trees?"

"It's been a while," he said with a chuckle, "since I talked to a tree, but you can talk to anything -- birds, clouds, even ants."

I guess I got what he meant. But practicing it was another thing. But after the dog incident, people said my dad was some kind of hero or saint. He could talk to animals. It was true, he really could. My dad had magically tamed a ferocious bulldog. Now the dog waited by the fence to *make friends with people*. All because of my dad.

I learned a lot that day.

The way I saw it, my dad treated everybody the same – people, animals, or insects. Whether downright mean or altogether nice – my dad treated them with the same attentive respect. And his soft, gentle way of dealing with the world came *straight from the heart*.

And that was just how the world treated him.

Cedar Run Farm
Westminster, Maryland (1950)

I grew up around cedars and swamps with *blue lies* flickering in the night. Some people said the *lies* were the work of *hants* and we weren't supposed to pay attention to them. Other people said they were just gas from the swamp given off by *humours*.

Downwind from the swamp was a farm owned by a man who was said to be a lot of trouble. His name was Whittaker Chambers, and though everybody read about him in the papers as an accomplice in a great Russian spy ring that included Alger Hiss, I knew nothing of this because I was five years old at the time.

But I knew whenever I heard the word *calmness*, people were talking about Mr. Chambers again. He was supposed to be both quiet and bad like the nightworkings of whatever it was lived in the swamp and made us see those blue lies.

Calmness. There was a great fear of this down on the farm. More people were more scared of calmnesses than all the hants and blue lies put together. But I had just gotten over my deepest fear -- *Gnatsies.*

Gnatsies were the soldiers from Germany who were made to work on our farm. They were gray ghosts, as far as I was concerned, wearing the dismal uniforms of defeat. The grays they wore reminded my mother's helper, Marie, of a story she'd heard from her mother who had been a slave.

I'd sit on Marie's lap and she's tell me stories. "Soldiers from a long-gone time once rode their horses right across this farm and watered their horses at the bottom of the hill where the swamp begins to give off them bluey lies. Maybe them lies was the spirits of the blues that took off after the grays."

I knew only the Gnatsies. They wore their grays every day. I'd not heard of these other blues and grays, and it was all very confusing to a five year old.

"Yanks, don't you know?" Marie went on to explain. "This land of your father's is built half on southern and half on northern. Nobody else has a farm so split up by the two sides."

She went on, as was her way of telling, about all the things I didn't know, while I listened to the rise and fall of her voice and studied the steam-burn she had on her chest.

I used to ask, time and again, if that steam-burn was made by the leeches down by the leeching pond before the swamp started. But, deep down, I was pretty sure the steam-burn was made by the blue lies, but she wouldn't confirm nor deny either of these notions.

One day, she said, "I'll tell it just so ... I got this here steam-burn doing other folkses ironing. That was just my carelessness working before I was old enough to know better and to know how to use a hot iron that was heated up on a wood stove."

For my part, I put all these stories and words into a special place in my head. That way I'd know what to do when steam-burns came at me, or the blue lies seeped out of the swamp, and of course, Gnatsies who might at any time rise up and kill us in our beds, which was the realest possibility of all, except that the Gnatsies were soon to be sent back to Germany wherever that was.

Calmness. No doubt this was the worst of the dangers we faced. I heard so many people talk about it. I remember waking in the middle of the night clutching my parakeet whose name was Treacherous Spaghetti (I always slept with Treacherous) and I'd hear a weird wind at the window. I wondered if this wind was calmness coming. After that, I thought about how Mr. Whittaker Chambers used this calmness to enter peoples' homes without really being seen.

I also wondered if Mr. Chambers might be able to lead a charge using the blue lies. They could sort of run ahead of him clearing the way, as imagined it. I wondered how the pumpkins might go along with the blue lies and Mr. Chambers.

The pumpkins were all laid out in a row when the men, who wore gray raincoats and must've been related to the older grays I'd heard about, came to cut them open. I had the feeling these new grays were cheap imitations of the old grays who had, according to Marie, a lot more dignity.

All the pretty pumpkins with their insides ripped open.

"Why did the grays do that?" I asked Marie.

"They was looking for the tapes hidden inside them pumpkins."

"What tapes?"

"The calmness tapes."

It seemed to me, hearing it this way, everything was all tied up together and all of it was about one thing doing a bad thing to another thing.

While I was listening to Marie, I got a new insight into the locality of the steam-burn. It stopped at the length and breadth of her bosom. So, I reasoned, she was just ironing the top part of her. Once I asked her, "How did you get all the brown off your palms?" Marie's palms were whitish-pink. She answered, "Too much ironing." So, it seemed to me she must've ironed herself pretty regularly, because it looked like some of her was lighter in color.

I had my lines pretty straight and if I added what I learned from my parents' parties, then I had a decent idea of what made the grownup world work the way it did. It was all very simple when you figured it out and got your lines straight. Everything wanted to do something, but not everything could. I felt that way myself. I had many things I wanted to do but couldn't do them yet.

The first thing I wanted to do was meet Mr. Chambers and talk pumpkins with him.

The second thing I wanted was to find out whether the old blues killed off the old grays, and whether they could only come back now as Gnatsie grays or these other grays in raincoats, the ones who ripped out the hearts of the pumpkins.

The third thing, I wanted to find out whether my father who said he liked Mr. Chambers was a calmness himself.

My five-year-old farm world was composed of so many mysteries, so many miracles.

If you eliminated one of these mysteries, you still had the others. And it seemed to me the real truth was you couldn't eliminate any and still not have all.

I had no way of knowing that Mr. Chambers was not going to lose more than a few pumpkins. I had no way of knowing then that he'd be jailed for his calmness ways. I also didn't realize that I'd never see him again, and so would never be able to talk to him.

When he was gone and I was old enough to understand the whole truth, all my five- year-old theories fell apart. Things weren't ever glued together so well they couldn't be hastily smashed like Mr. Chambers' pumpkins.

As I got older still, I also learned that gray was better than blue -- unless of course the opposite was true, which it sometimes proved to be, as in the case of my parakeet, Treacherous Spaghetti. Orange was OK -- unless you were a pumpkin. Black was sometimes dangerous because of the steam-burns and ironing. Red was bad, plain bad, and even the Gnatsies weren't that bad. Red was calmness, and wicked.

In the end, like all kids, I decided it was more fun to pick up war souvenirs in the form of brass buttons with eagles on them. These were scattered all over the Union Road that led to someplace called Gettysburg where there was a big gray and blue battle going on. The way I heard it, it was an old battle, but one that would never quit. Even the calmness and the Gnatsies couldn't hold a candle to the gray blue battle. I may be 68 years old now, but I can attest to that.

GLOSSARY

Blue Lies: Blue lights caused by escaping swamp gas

Hants: Ghosts

Humours: Vapors once thought to be harmful

Calmness: Communist

Gnatsies: Nazis

Old Grays: Confederates

Old Blues: Yankees

Grays in raincoats: Federal agents

Leeching Pond: swampy water where blood sucking leeches were imagined to breed, but also, a leeching pond can be a sewage drainage area.

Treacherous Spaghetti: pasta unfit to eat or rather a parakeet with that same name.

Whittaker Chambers: Journalist and editor accused of conspiring to sell secrets to Russia in the 1940s. He was later cleared of any wrong doing, but Alger Hiss who was also implicated was proven to be a spy.

Pumpkins: Actual farm grown pumpkins on Chambers' farm. One of the pumpkins contained microfilm documents of espionage intent.

Buttons: Hard to believe but in the 1940s on the dirt road by our farmhouse there were buttons and other bits of metal from that most famous of all Civil War battles.

674 Plainfield Avenue
Berkeley Heights, New Jersey (1952)

A friend said, "You haven't lived until you have died."

Now if I hadn't really respected this friend, I don't think I would've tried it ... dying, I mean. It sounds crazy, I know. Even crazier when you consider what my mom said -- she said I came out laughing. That is, I was born laughing not crying. And I've been laughing ever since, so why should I want to try dying?

I can't answer that.

But this is what I did. It was dusk and I decided to visit my friend who has the name same as I do. He lives across the street. I stood there for a moment by the side of the road. It was a summer night and the cars were passing slowly. I looked at Gerry's front porch and his whole family was there. His mom and dad and two brothers.

I wanted to be on that porch so bad. It was night over there on account of the big oak that added shade to the coming darkness. They had candles on the porch and they were drinking ice tea. I looked to my left and then to my right. On my right a car was coming up Plainfield Avenue. It slowed and then sped up as it went by me. On the left a big Packard appeared and it was going fast. Can I outrun you? I asked myself. And my self said, Sure just take off on those super Keds sneakers. Run on the balls of your feet. GO!

I took off. The Packard picked up speed and came clanking down the street.

I'm going to make it, I'm going to make it.

I didn't make it.

The Packard ran over me in the middle of the road, right on the white line. I felt the front bumper strike my left knee, then it knocked me down and ran over me. The last thing I remember is the stink of oil underneath the Packard.

For a while I was dead. Or maybe I just thought I was. I floated off. I became light as air and I rose in the setting sun and at the same time I saw myself lying down on the road, but there was no blood. Dead with no blood? I had always expected lots of blood. Gallons of it. No blood, no body, no feeling about much of anything, just colors in the sky as I went higher and higher and the Packard got smaller and smaller.

And then I was back down there on the road and Gerry's mom was saying, "Is he alive?"

Yes of course I am alive, I said. Or thought I said.

Gerry's dad carried me across the street. My eyes were open by then. I felt OK. My body wasn't crushed. The Packard driver was waved off, and he drove away. The night was darker on this side of the road. Maybe I am dead, I said, because this feels weird.

Weirder still ... no one was crying. No wailing. No emergency phone calls to the hospital. Nothing. Gerry's dad just lay me out on that gray board porch. I heard him say, "He's stunned but not hurt." How did he know? I still wasn't so sure. I thought I might be dead and just seeing all this stuff with my mind.

Or my soul. Or whatever it is that lives after you die; I was never sure about that.

After a little while my parents showed up. My dad felt every part of my body. He had been a medical student before he became a mechanical engineer and he knew some things about broken bones.

"Gerry," he said softly, "are you all right?"

My tongue suddenly loosened up. "I'm fine. The car just rolled over me but I was in between the tires and they didn't touch me."

I'm going to stop talking about this right now because it's bringing back some funny memories. Like, why was everyone so calm? Didn't they know I'd just died and left my body and gone off into the sky and come back and re-entered my body? Sure I was all right, but didn't they want to know about where I'd just been?

No one cared. Well, my parents did. But when I finally was able to express what an amazing thing dying was, they shrugged it off, and my mom said, "Gerry, you have the world's most active imagination and one day you're going to be a writer!"

She was right about that, of course. But to tell the truth, and I am doing that in this story right now, I have never shared this with anyone. This is the first time. I know everybody says that. But, believe me, I never did share this particular story with anyone. There is a reason. I was never sure it happened the way I thought it did.

Can humans really fly? Is there such a thing as a soul and does it do the flying? Do we sometimes fly at night when we sleep? Do we leave our body resting and fly off into ...wherever we go when we dream?

After that night I began a series of experiments using my Self as a witness.

This, then, is the story about how I learned how to fly.

But that is only one of the things I learned to do ... I also learned to see ghosts, talk to them, stay under water for long periods of time, fall in love with girls, meet beings from other realms, see into the future, but most of all, I learned how to fly. Stay with me for a while and I'll tell you about it.

None of this is made up.

*

So I survived being run over ... and it was not long before I survived the memory of it. Only now, thinking back, do I remember again the floating up over the world that I knew so well.

When I dreamed after the accident, I was always in the early evening, floating above the little town where I lived.

Several things happened next that changed my life.

First, I jumped out of my bedroom window on the second floor of our house. I threw my arms out like a bird, and flew without flapping. Just flew.

For a few seconds it seemed so anyway. Then I plummeted to the earth.

Miraculously I landed standing up, then I tucked and rolled. And was standing again.

Once more, a miracle occurred. I was all right. I looked up at the open window in the second story attic of our house.

What had happened? Had I really jumped into the air expecting to fly? Had I flown?

I knew but one thing in that moment. I was unhurt.

Then I ran back into the house and went through the kitchen where my mother was preparing breakfast. I went up the narrow stairs into the attic where I shared a bedroom with my brother. The window was open -- and just like that -- I leaped out of it, soared through the air again, turned upside down, then right-side up, and landed on the balls of my feet. I stood straight up for an eye-blink. Then I dived and rolled and stood again.

After that I lay down in the soft grass of summer and laughed.

And laughed.

I was unbreakable.

I was Miracle Boy.

I could do miraculous things.

I proceeded to do them.

One after another...

Point Brielle
South Jersey (1959)

Monday's child is fair of face
Tuesday's child is full of grace
Wednesday's child is full of woe
Thursday's child has far to go
Friday's child is loving and giving
Saturday's child works hard for his living
And the child that is born on Sabbath day
Is bonny and blithe and good and gay

Mother Goose Nursery Rhyme

I failed my dive test and had to take it over again.

I'd done the same thing with my driver's test. I failed that because I didn't know how to release the clutch of a standard shift 1960 Ford Fairlane on a wet, steep hill. I revved and released suddenly and the big car bunny-hopped, slid sideways on the wet pavement. I wound up on somebody's lawn.

My dive test was even worse; I nearly drowned.

The thing is, you can easily forget good advice if you're half-listening which was a bad habit of mine when I was growing up.

My dive instructor was a crabby old Navy SEAL instructor. He had white eyebrows, and that's about all I remember except the following which I have painfully reconstructed. The man said to me, very gruffly, "I want you to remove all of your dive equipment in the following manner. First, take off your fins. Then take off your tank, but keep the petcock open so you can breathe. Place the tank beside the fins, and keep breathing normally. Take a deep breath of oxygen, and hold it. Turn the valve off. Take off your weight belt. Remove your mask. Swim to the surface."

The order of this procedure is paramount to success. You need air to breathe until the ascent. You must have your weight belt on while you are breathing air. If not, you could shoot to the surface too quickly and risk air embolism, which is also called the bends. At fifty feet, this matters. At ten feet it doesn't matter that much, but even at that depth, if you rise too fast with lungs full of surface air from a dive tank, it feels like you got kicked in the chest.

Suffice to say, I doffed in the wrong order. I kept my weight belt on right to the end and held my air because I was rooted to the bottom. We were in about twenty feet of clear water, and I was stuck down there, and couldn't get to the surface because I have what my instructor called "sinker's bones." Heavy boned, he meant. Real heavy, and with the weight belt on and no air, I was meat. Dead meat. Gulp of water, and I was a goner.

You run out of oxygen, all kinds of things happen.

I could see the man up top doing hand signals which meant – "Open the valve on your tank, breathe normally." But sadly, I'd taken off my mask and I was nearsighted, so even a few feet away, my instructor was blurry.

Once again, suffice to say, I failed the test.

However, I took it again and this time the instructor gave me thumbs up and I got my scuba license.

On my first big dive, I knew the rules but once again, I wasn't paying attention to them.

Cardinal rule in diving -- always dive with a partner.

I ignored the importance of that rule.

So my first dive went awry.

Following the gradient slant of the underwater slope of beige sand, I allowed myself to go down to where the saltwater got colder and greener and blacker. Soon it was twilight down there. I went deeper. And heard a sound -- *whirla-whirla-wicka-wicka*, and so on.

Turning my head, then my entire body, I rotated 360 degrees.

Saw nothing but the dark silk fabric of the bay.

And that was the weird thing.

Point Brielle – pretty name for a dead body of water. I was about 45 feet down just hanging and waiting to see something while I listened to the muffled noise. Visibility dimmed, clouded. The bottom got grayer, muckier; and the deeper I went, the inkier it got.

Way deep down was ground zero for grundge.

Then I saw something my mind refused to believe.

The backdrop I'd been staring at was the haunted mist of Brielle Bay. But now this backdrop, faintly sun-spoked when I first entered, turned black as night. Even my foreground was shadowy. Startled whitefish, wide-eyed, shot past me. What was happening?

The backdrop of darkness transformed into a monster shape that I decided must be a whale. If that were so, I was but a few feet away from it. The whale sucked me closer to its rivets.

Rivets?

Then I discovered what I was seeing.

The side of a very big ship. An oil tanker maybe. Rusted ancient steel plate went past me and I could feel a strange force drawing me ever closer to the ship's hull.

I was being drawn closer and closer to a huge propeller.

I could see it turning. The silt and sand was like an underwater dust-devil. It was growing darker by the second.

And then –

--nothing.

Just a moil of oil and a swirl of sand.

My oxygen was about gone.

I glanced overhead and saw a tiny daystar sun on the surface, and I kicked upward with my fins. The mirror of the bright surface above me gleamed with hope and promise. I kept kicking for all I was worth.

At last I surfaced. Now I was but a few feet away from the rusted tanker.

"What you see down there?" a shirtless man yelled from the deck.

"Nothing much," I said. "What do you see up there?"

"Whole lot of sharks," he said, pointing to the stern of the ship. "They get meat rot from the galley when we dock."

Without my glasses on, I couldn't see the curved fins carving the starboard chum.

Without a moment's hesitation, I swam to shore and was thankful as hell the sharks didn't see me. But I've often wondered what would've happened if I'd been born on Tuesday rather than Thursday. Tuesday's child is full of grace. But, as we know, Thursday's child has far to go.

And now I knew just how far that was.

Rattlesnake Mountain Road
Stockbridge, Massachusetts (1963)

I was driving my dad's 1957 Ford station wagon on Rattlesnake Mountain Road outside of Stockbridge, Massachusetts.

I wanted to be a folksinger -- and there on this twilit country road was a tall man and a short man, walking. I recognized the tall guy immediately and slowed the car. I was keeping pace with them for a moment. The tall one was Pete Seeger, the shorter one was twelve-string guitar master, Bob Davenport from England.

I pulled the station-wagon over to the side of the road. I got out and walked over to Pete and said, "You mind if I walk with you?" It was brazen, and foolish. Pete looked at Davenport with less than a smile and more of a question mark. Davenport whispered, "I'd like to know what they're thinking, these American kids." Pete turned to me and said, "Come along then." I waved to my cousin Kyle and she got behind the wheel and drove off ... and I was alone with a legend and the legend's friend, who was really the one permitting the walk-along-side.

In my memory that walk lasted forty hours. But whatever time it took walking the length of it and then coming back and walking another length was sweet to me because these two great musicians were talking about everything under the sun. And then -- after the real sun sank behind Monument Mountain, Pete made that statement I'll never forget: "If you squeezed that mountain the sap would run out and turn into culture." I knew what he meant -- the Berkshires of Massachusetts was the heartland of New England poetry, prose and let's not forget maple syrup. The way Pete said it, and explained it, the dripping sap off that mountain contained the souls of Hawthorne, Melville, Thoreau, Stowe, Sedgwick, Bryant, Longfellow and all the rest.

After a while we sat down in a field and counted fireflies. I'll never forget that night. Nor will I forget, some years later meeting another folk legend, Ray Brock who gave me a pancake recipe that he liked to use in the Virgin Islands on a Baltic ketch, "and don't forget the fresh nutmeg" -- and I never do, Ray!

All this may seem like a long time gone, to me it's the wink of a firefly on a summer's night.

The Gaslight Cafe
Greenwich Village, NYC (1964)

I was in my favorite hangout, Minetta Tavern in Greenwich Village.

I had just seen Bob Dylan, up close and personal, you might say, at the Gaslight Cafe on Macdougal.

Dylan was a kid, just like me, and nobody that night was paying much attention to him as he pounded his way through his adapted version of *Red Rockin' Chair*, an Appalachian ballad, more of a bluegrass number. I looked at Dylan in his beaten-up suede jacket and his 1930s Depression era cap and he was scruffier than I was and looked quite a bit younger. Not too many people that night were listening to him, so he sort of sang to me, or so I thought.

Minetta's was a cool place and my friend Jimmy MacFadyen and I ate there often.

Jimmy was writing a novel called *The Travels of Jaimie MacFadyen* because he'd busked about the country living in a boxcar with country singer Hoyt Axton whose mother wrote the song *Blue Suede Shoes* popularized by Elvis. My friend Jimmy knew a lot of folksingers. "If we put our minds to it," he said, "we could meet lots of people on the folk circuit and then we could write about them and become famous in our own right."

Jimmy had a big ego, but he was on to something. I'd already met Reverend Gary Davis, the blues and gospel singer, and he'd told us some funny stories and I could remember them. I told myself that even before our spaghetti and meatballs arrived, I was going to write a story about the good old Reverend. But right after we ate, Jimmy and I headed back to the Gaslight where Dylan was done, and we met Ramblin Jack Elliott walking in the front door with a pretty girl under each arm and his guitar slung across his back. For some reason, the great rambler liked us. Maybe because we liked him.

Anyway he sang *Tennessee Stud* because we asked him to and then he dedicated a couple more songs to our "youth and enthusiasm brimming all over the place" and everyone looked over to see the brimmers. Afterwards I went home and wrote a story about Jack and another one about Reverend Gary. I showed these to the editor of our school newspaper and he said, "Sure, we'll publish them but who in hell are these guys?"

It was then I realized that fame was a matter of perception. Then Jimmy called me and said, "Bob Dylan's back in town. We should interview him. You know, he'll probably end up being the most famous folksinger of them all." I wondered how that was possible -- that little guy with the hoarse voice nobody listened to?

"Dylan's got this friend named Alan Aronowitz who got him to come and stay at Free Acres. Let's go over there and meet him."

Free Acres was a kind of old style 1920s kibbutz-like community where such famous people as the actor James Cagney and the writer MacKinlay Kantor had lived there and also the Romany writer Konrad Bercovici. I made a note to write about them, too.

Dylan wasn't very talkative. He was supposedly writing a song about a tambourine. That's what Aronowitz said. The only personal thing we learned about Dylan is that he ate scrambled eggs for dinner and he looked younger than Jimmy and me and maybe didn't shave much because he had nothing much to shave.

Back in the Village, the following weekend, we met Buffy Sainte-Marie. She was friendly enough and she sang *Now That The Buffalo's Gone* and the drive of her lyrics worked into the memoir I was writing.

Then Jimmy and I got really lucky. We stayed up all night and got to hear Dave Van Ronk sing his version of WB Yeats' poem *The Song of Wandering Aengus* about the trout that turns into a sort of fairy goddess, and the way Van Ronk sang -- all husky and smoky-voiced -- "The golden apples of the sun and the silver apples of the moon", well, his words followed us all the way back home to Berkeley Heights, New Jersey.

My intention to write a memoir about people I really didn't know stopped short the following morning. I glanced at my manuscript and threw the pages in the trash.

Van Ronk had done me a great service when he sang the WB Yeats poem. It was a bardic echo from the ancient past and it stuck with Jimmy and me. The following year I went to college. I studied modern English poetry. Jimmy didn't go to college. He stayed home and did drugs. A few years later it killed him. The folk era was over by that time. Folk music as we knew it morphed folk into folk rock. Van Ronk stayed the same, Dylan re-invented music altogether, all by himself.

As I say, Jimmy was gone and I still miss him. His sly smile, his passion for folk. I saw Van Ronk a few more times and met up with Jack Elliott in Tesuque, New Mexico with his dog Buttermilk. I wrote poetry and published it. I wrote about Jack, and published that. Maybe I'd never come up to Yeats' big toe or Dylan's boot heel, but that didn't matter: I was a published writer, wasn't I? I still search for Jimmy's novel, *The Travels of Jaimie MacFadyen* somewhere up there on some bookstore's long gone, lonesome traveler shelf, somewhere up there near to heaven

The Fat Black Pussycat
Greenwich Village, NYC (1964)

The good Reverend Gary Davis, a blind man who could see, told the people how it was, how it was going to be and he laid the notes down on his six-string guitar, an instrument that he played in his sleep -- not figuratively but really.

Few people, if any, were listening to the wizard of the six, who was doing a two-finger punch and strum and pick, and talking about the Twelve Gates to the City and other things that no one could hear because they were all talking, smoking and sipping and not listening.

Reverend Gary Davis faced the crowd, and listening or not, he addressed them with scorn:

"Some of you people don't realize it, taking the world by storm, don't even know how to treat your family…doing all kinds of ways…living all kinds of lives…saying everything in front of your children…ashes to ashes and dust to dust…the life you're living won't do to trust."

We left Reverend Gary while he was hammering his sermon, and we stopped by the Gaslight Cafe where a scruffy little guy with a big Martin guitar was pounding out a song called "Masters of War."

"Looks like Bob Dylan," someone said.

"It *is* Bob Dylan," someone answered.

When I think about those days and nights haunting the Village or rather, the Village haunting us, I often see the old black gospel singer from the Delta, a huge legend to many of us and then again I see the fog-voiced, hard-bitten midwestern kid with the dark blue sailor's cap and the wind blowing behind him as he shuffled those same folk-begotten streets we did.

They were two American prophets -- one going out, the other coming in.

But that one night they were one.

They were saying the same things -- their lives might be separated by age, color, geography, generation – but no more than that, and that, in itself, was nothing. To us anyway. They were two great heroes of the Greenwich Village folk singing night.

It was 1964 and the summer was heating up and everyone was talking about civil rights and the John Birch Society and the Vietnam War was about to happen and no one that I knew was reading a novel called *Appointment in Samarra* by John O'Hara and I kept hearing Reverend Gary's corn husk, old man's rasp voice:

"Ashes to ashes, dust to dust, the life you're living won't do to trust."

The Veeder Building, South Pacific Avenue, Old Town Las Vegas, New Mexico (1967)

It was like a deer stalk the way he came after me. He knew where I was. You don't need to know any of the rest. He was given a certain amount of time to kill me. I complied, by staying alive and him stalked me, scented me, sensed me, ran me over on his motorcycle on a cold dark night.

I remember his face. I will always remember his face. He was the wolf; I was the deer. He stayed there for a little while, curious to see me close. He reassured himself that he'd done what he'd come to do. I lay there bleeding to death in the broken glass and the moon.

The thing about a near death experience is the way you process it. You see flashes from your former life, the life you lived when you were whole. Then, after that, you see images of the night, of darkness. These play with your mind -- the furred face of the wolf, its wolfen smell, canus lupus fragrance of death.

There was the river, too, the scent of swiftly moving water, the canyon, the perpendicular rock walls, the scented ponderosa pines, the wind coming all the way from Johnson Mesa and moaning into the Gallinas Canyon and the golden dung of horses giving off their straw and the stink of goats and the cold rusty mineral smell of cold rock and dried blood.

In my mind, now, I see the white incisors, the wolfen eyes of inquiry, the predatory glare -- are you dead yet? The face hangs over me, furred and famished, framed by a bad moon on the canyon rim. Blood moon on cold lichen, penitenté moon on piñon pine.

You process it, over time. You reach out for it, piece by piece and put it together until it seems to make sense. Someone out there in the world, the real world, wants you dead. A wolf stalks a deer, kills it. Hunts it, drinks its blood. I am the autumn deer. You are the wolf. I die by degrees into winter. You live in your footprints.

And wake to the moon faces of my Navajo friends, Joogii DeGroat and Jimmie Blueeyes. Their silent vigil, by my bedside, singing the Blessingway, putting me back together, piece by piece like the ant people when the Hero Twin was struck by lightning.

The months follow one another.

"What did you do with my gun?" my brother asks one day.

"I keep it under my pillow."

"Don't shoot yourself in the head."

"I won't."

Uncle Milty comes in a little after this. He drops off a shopping bag, a gift. He says some funny things and then, just for the hell of it, he draws the face of Jesus on my cast. I look at it in the mirror. It's the most believable face I've ever seen. It resembles the image on the Shroud of Turin only Milty's Jesus doesn't look like a misplaced Viking who's asking God, "How did I get here?"

The Jesus face Milty drew on me was like me. Full of pain, all broken up, run-over, cast aside, dismembered, shot, confused, slammed, time out of mind busted luck pain. I respected Milty for his great artwork but what was I going to do with a shopping bag full of weed when all I wanted was blood?

I sat up all night with my gun listening to a Morman elder on the radio: "Help the weak if you are strong, come out and be strong and confess your truth," he said. I talked to the elder hidden in the radio and babbled my madness into the twin speakers while I fingered my gun and cocked the hammer and levered it back down, and cocked it again.

I imagined stalking the hit-and-run guy who'd almost killed me. This image dissolved and I heard Joogii DeGroat and Jimmie Blueeyes, chanting. I heard a wolf howl. I put my brother's gun away in a drawer. I wrote a single sentence in my notebook --

"We humans fear the beast within the wolf because we do not

understand the beast within ourselves."

University and 5th
Las Vegas, New Mexico (1968)

In that cursed or blessed year of the dragon, I was run over by a motorcyclist. Long story short, I almost bled to death in a narrow canyon. The guy who hit me was drunk and just back from Vietnam and he had no headlight. Leave it at that, and the fact I was in the hospital for weeks and then recovering for months, and you have the cursed year of the dragon. The blessed year, I'll tell you about in a minute. It was the same year though.

The dragon year brought an actual dragon into our house. My brother caught it in a cave in Mexico and brought it to me in a large terrarium with a screened top so the thing couldn't get away. Let me tell you, it was ugly. Dark brown, thick tailed, gape mouthed, well-toothed ugly. I was scared of it, though it was relatively small, about two feet long and quite fat. I never fed it anything. It never wanted to eat, as far as I could tell. What it wanted to do was bite. That gave me the jitters because, as I said, I was damaged goods as a result of the hit-and-run. Did I mention that the motorcyclist left me right after he crushed every bone in my right leg? I was bleeding all over the place ... but now I'm getting away from my story or maybe I should say it's getting away from me.

Back to the dragon. While recuperating, I used to sort of camp out in the living room and have staring contests with the creature. It was pure perversity on my part because if it ever got out of the thick glass tank it was in, I would've been dead meat instead of damaged goods. That's how I felt anyway.

My brother came in one day and saw the staring contest and said, "I caught that rascal so you would feel safe and now I see you like to play with fire."

"The only thing it does is look at me. I look back. Hey, I have nothing else to do. But sometimes I wonder what would happen if it ever got out."

"You'd be helpless, I guess."

My brother was like that. Life was just a bunch of alternatives to him. But I guess we're all like that. But then, my alternative was this: I needed some back up. I had a cat that might've stood a chance against the dragon. A really big cat. Also a gift from my brother.

But it was a hearty, go-off-and-get-laid male cat who was seldom at home. As fate would have it though, after my brother left, the cat came back.

That night I fell asleep on the floor in my sleeping bag and the dragon nosed his way to the screen and drove himself hard and upright. They can do that, you know. They can stand upright like a little man. This one could anyway. And did. And I woke up early in the morning and the great big tom was having a staring contest with the fat, ugly dark, leathery dragon. I smelled the faint fragrance of incense or smoke.

The cat was named Fangclamp because that was one of the things he did best. He was as large as a bobcat and weighed close to thirty pounds, most of it meat and bone, no fat.

Fangclamp and the dragon were about five feet apart when I woke. The cat's lantern-like green eyes were fixed on the dragon's spiteful gold eyes. Neither one moved. Or twitched. They just stared.

"Do something," I told the cat.

Fangclamp shuddered once, the way cats do. A ripple of a twitch and he was gone. The way cats do: disappear like smoke. I smelled it, too, not cat smoke. But that other dragon smoke or whatever it was.

My brother came to see me a few hours later. I hadn't moved an inch. Neither had the dragon. I started wondering if it liked me. My brother, letting himself in with his own key, stood at the front door. He took in the scene, left abruptly, came back with a wire fishnet which he threw over the dragon. The creature didn't struggle or anything. My brother dragged it to the holding tank, a two-hundred-gallon job (empty of water of course because this was a land dragon) and dropped the dragon in and quickly laid on the screen topper.

"This isn't going to work," he said, holding the topper down with his hand. "The thing's going to bust out again. So, you got any heavy, I mean really heavy books?"

"I've got a hardcover volume of Chaucer and another of collected Shakespeare plays and the two together probably weigh about forty pounds."

I nodded toward the bookcase and my brother selected the leather-bound books and put them down on the topper.

"What's that smell?" he said.

"Dragon shit. I don't know."

He shrugged. "If he gets out again, I'm taking him back."

"You can take me back too," I told him.

"Where to?"

"To the hospital."

He shrugged and left. He was that way. I knew he loved me but he had a funny way of showing it.

That afternoon my friend Joogii came by. Joogii's the son of a Navajo medicine man and he took one look at the dragon and said, "Pichiquatay."

"Is that Navajo?" I asked him.

"No. It's Mexican. Actually it's Mayan."

"What's it mean?"

"Dragon lizard."

"You've seen one before?"

"One time. My father said these are good medicine when they take another form. But, like this, the way you see it. It brings bad luck."

"He already chased my cat away. I don't think he likes me. He's got very sharp teeth."

Joogii said, "What makes you think the dragon's a he?"

I was still thinking about that when he told me it was female.

"In this form," he said, "right now, Pichiquatay is dangerous. You'd better get rid of her. But be gentle. If she gets angry or even upset, you might get hurt."

"I'm already pretty banged up," I said. "I have twelve breaks below the knee and I probably won't walk normally for the rest of my life. What more could the dragon do?"

Joogii smiled faintly. "Plenty," he said.

Before he left, he asked, "Where's that cat, Clamp?"

"He went out."

Joogii laughed. "Tell him not to come back. They like cat's meat, Pichiquatays."

"How about human meat?"

His smile vanished. "Only the bones."

He stood by the door. I might not see him again for months. "So, before you leave, old friend, tell me something."

He nodded. "All right."

"What's the so-called 'good medicine' you mentioned?"

"Oh, that. That's when they turn into a mud puppy. That's the good medicine. A real blessing."

I scratched my head. "How do you get 'em to turn?"

He chuckled. "You can't. But if you should see a mud puppy somewhere, it could be this one. And that would be a blessing. Your leg could heal real fast then."

The next morning when I woke up, the dragon was gone. He'd, I mean, she'd, chewed through all of Chaucer and half of Shakespeare. My brother came and looked all over the house and that pichi was one gone cat! And that reminds me -- Fangclamp never returned.

Two months later I was strapped into a leg brace of chrome and leather and steel with a Florsheim shoe at the bottom. I limped along pretty good, but my leg still wasn't healing and the surgeon who'd put me back together said he was afraid I had osteomyelitis, which means you don't really ever heal. Sometimes they just excise the leg. That's how he put it. "Eat plenty of yogurt," he said.

One day a week or so after that my brother took me to Storrie Lake outside of town. There was a small man with a large straw on and he caught a fish and started yelling, "Pichiquatay." You better believe I hobbled over there.

The man was terrified of the thing flopping on the other end of his line. He dropped his pole and began praying. Then I knew he wasn't terrified, but instead, overawed. As if he was seeing the Second Coming. My brother said, "He keeps saying dragon."

"This is the other form they take," I told him. "The good form. This is a blessing."

We freed the creature from the hook and he wiggled away. He was almost the same size as the dragon but this one had feathery-looking gills and a round, funny head like a puppy dog. Harmless looking thing ... but weird as all hell, too. His front feet resembled human hands.

After that day at Storrie Lake my leg healed rapidly. I told my doc it was the yogurt. But he said it was a medical miracle.

Just the other night I chanced to be working on a script in Quebec, Canada, and I looked across the St. Lawrence river at eventide. As the sun disappeared behind the Laurentians, a raindrop fell from the sky, one raindrop of dark blue dragon's blood ...

Quebec, you are a dragon, an old curled-up but dead one. You got scared before you died and the sweat popped out of your hide and froze bright white, Quebec. Seeing the dragon, fully exposed, fully, geographically blossomed, I understood the dragon was not one thing, but something much larger. It was the whole year, the year of the dragon.

Writing

Ilfeld Auditorium, New Mexico Highlands University
Las Vegas, New Mexico (1966)

I read *The Gypsy Ballads of Federico Garcia Lorca* fifty-two years ago and I've been carrying them in my head ever since. Sometimes I wake and they are there. Myrtle and lime. Three hundred crimson roses. Trails of tears and tin lights and the moon swimming in sounding water. And then I come to these unforgettable lines resonating lines ringing in my head:

> *Green as I would have you be.*
> *Green wind. Green boughs.*
> *The boat on the sea*
> *And the horse on the mountain*

I remember reciting these lines to my professor, Dr. Richard O'Connell, translator with James-Graham Lujan of *Five Plays* by Lorca, and he smiled. "Whose translation is that?" he asked.

I told him, "Rolfe Humphries."

Doc, as we called him, looked a little uneasy. "Rolfe will forgive me if I say he got it wrong. It needs to be more like, 'Green, green, I want you green.'"

He emphasized it with his hands, clasping the air, grabbing at the invisible but palpable green. "Maybe desire is a better word than want," he said. "Have you heard it better?" he asked. "Maybe I said, and I recited:

> *Green green rocky road*
> *promenade in green*
> *Tell me who you love*
> *Tell me who you love*

"That isn't Lorca!" Doc said.

"It's Len Chandler, folksinger-poet. I heard him sing his green song at The Gaslight in Greenwich Village in 1962. Len played the 12 string and he could really get you going with that song. Bob Dylan was usually in the audience."

"Who's that?" Doc asked.

Maurice Sendak's Studio
Ridgefield, Connecticut (1973)

We visited Maurice in the Fall after Ruth Krauss (bestselling author of *A Hole Is To Dig*) introduced him to us. Of all the crazy things -- we were re-publishing two books of theirs. That is, classic children's books written by nutty, witty Ruth and master pen-and-inker, Maurice. How the two of them linked up is interesting.

Ruth "discovered" Maurice, as she put it, when he was a department window-dresser in Manhattan. As she also put it, "He was really just a kid." What was it she saw in that window? We never found out, but I think it can be summed up in one word -- genius.

Well, anyway, we became publishers, thanks to Ruth and courtesy of Maurice whom she always called Maury. The books of theirs we loved and reprinted lovingly were *Somebody Else's Nut Tree* and also *I'll Be You and You Be Me*.

Our partner in this endeavor was David Silverstein who owned The Bookstore, which was a few steps away from The Restaurant in Lenox, Massachusetts. David had a sense of humor. So did Ruth. She thought it was pretty funny that her books with Maurice were out of print. We got them back into print. We had no money. We made a deal with a printer, Tom Reardon, who made a deal with his brothers and father, and the presses began rolling.

Two years later, we had two bestselling children's books selling for $1.95 a copy.

I remember driving down to Ridgefield, Connecticut to see Maurice about having him sign a limited edition in hardcover. Naturally we brought our daughter Mariah, age 3, along with us. Even as we entered Maurice's front door, Mariah asked, "Is this the house of Ruth?"

"No," I said it's the house of Maurice." (I never called him Maury, he didn't like the name even when Ruth used it.)

"Does he do the Nut Tree?" Mariah asked.

"Yes, And also the Wild Things."

"Oh, she said.

In Maurice's house there is a room chock full of Mickeys. As you might expect, Mariah loved Mickey Mouse and immediately believed that this magical Maurice with the pen knew Mickey quite well.

Maurice signed the limited editions and then he asked Mariah, whose mouth was still open as she studied the many Mickeys, "Would you like an apple from my apple tree?"

"Is it a nut tree?" Mariah asked.

"It's an apple tree," Maurice said. He'd about had it, I could tell. Not with us, with her. She wasn't paying attention to him. Not at all. Just the Mickeys. So he offered something that made my heart jump. He said, "Would you like a Wild Thing?"

Mariah's eyes revolved around the Mickey clocks with their white-gloved hands. Finally she looked at Maurice, but she still didn't say anything. That was when he gave her an apple from his tree and at the same time sat down and drew a really wild looking Wild Thing.

Mariah stood very close to him, but gradually her eyes went from Maurice's facile pen-hand to the closest Mickey clock. "Hey, kid," Maurice said, "I don't do Wild Things for just anybody. I have a big ego, pay attention to me!"

Mariah obeyed, if a bit reluctantly. Maurice finished the drawing with a little flourish and an inscription to Mariah from her friend Maurice Sendak. Mariah took a big bite of the apple and a huge drop of juice came off her lip and landed smack on Maurice's drawing.

Maurice laughed.

On the way home, Mariah, still eating Maurice's apple, said, "That Ruth Krauss was nice."

New Marlboro Road
Monterey, Massachusetts (1973)
State Road 22
Tesuque, New Mexico (1979)

I always wrote poems for the children. My children, Hannah and Mariah. But other children, too. The children I'd visit at schools in different parts of the country.

The first poem I wrote for Mariah who was born in July, 1971, was about her sock. We were camping in the old family cabin at Lake Buel in the Berkshires in Massachusetts.

It was night and I had just lit the kerosene lantern. The cabin had no electricity, no water, a very primitive little knothole of a place but we loved it. This night the darkness swarmed the pine woods. There was just the kerosene lantern and the darkness.

Lorry said, "Mariah's missing one sock."

So I went outside in the dark. The smell of damp pine, no stars, no moon. Just night.

I stood barefoot on pine needles. My feet the only white thing in all that night-ness.

And then I saw it. All by itself. A tiny white sock.

I picked it up and held it like a treasure. It was no longer, no wider, than my thumb.

I felt a tear run down my cheek. I don't know what it was – the tiny sock or the discovery of it, or both. We were very poor that summer and one sock was oh-so-important, especially in that moment.

And then I heard a barred owl call from a dead pine.

Lorry called from the porch, "Find it?"

"Found it."

Four and a half years later, Mariah used to go on owl walks with me. By then we were living in a 150-year-old colonial farmhouse, with no heat or water. We were getting good at roughing it. Maybe we preferred it that way.

I dug a shallow well that went dry in August. Then I carried buckets of water from our kind neighbor Harold. Our liberation from the stress of day was, once again, the glory of nightfall. The night I am remembering, I wrote my second Mariah Poem. The first was the baby sock.

Mariah & the Owls

Out at twilight, listening for owls,
my daughter and me.
She rides upon my shoulders
the way the moon rides
the bare haunch of a deer.

Listen, do you hear?
One sound plaited upon another.
Darkness, the Shadow Weaver.

Moon whinnies on the hillside
but no owls.
The bellow of a distant cow,
cars, creaking branches, far off dogs
barking but no owls.

Then it comes: a shrilly whimper
one and then another
and that is all.
A young screech owl has flown
home to its mate
with a mouse in its claws.

I stand up. Cold sneakers,
rush of blood returning to my body.
The weight on my shoulders
is sound asleep and snoring.

Mariah, did you hear? Silence.
The walk home, and then I put
her to bed, clothes and all.
She blinks in the glare of a table light.

"Daddy," she says, at once wide awake,
"I heard that owl," and falls back asleep.

In the summer of 1976 our second daughter, Hannah, was born.

I remember walking up the stairs to the hospital with Lorry whose water had not broken but we knew it was maybe moments away.

As we went up the long trajectory of stairs, so very slowly, I thought: in this moment my wife is both a young woman and an old woman. She walked with a decided stoop.

Coming down the stairs was a real old woman. I stared at her for a moment and realized she was, in fact, my great aunt Edith. She was, I knew, one year shy of 100.

She saw me and I saw her and we had a small celebration on the stairs. "You better get going," she advised, nodding at Lorry's belly with happy approval.

Hannah was born with that blessing.

One year later, we were on the road moving back to New Mexico. Hannah had her first birthday in Tesuque where we were going to build an adobe house.

That summer Hannah's first words came tumbling out of her mouth. Cactus was Kakees. Snow was Ock (her word for milk). There was still snow on Santa Fe Baldy and Hannah called it ock and I loved to hear her say it. I carried her up into the high mountains to see the ock. She sat in a backpack and she'd lean left or right, and I'd feel myself falling, catching my balance just in time.

Later, Hannah was singing in the car.

Lorry was driving and she had a long red thick braid. Hannah was playfully holding and shaking it like a maraca while she made up

verses that had a blues beat:
"Mama has a big hair
She don't know!
Mama has a big hair
She don't know!"

Hannah was a child of dance and song, right from the start.

One afternoon Lorry put the fresh bread in the bread drawer that was at the bottom of the hutch in the kitchen.

Hannah danced on the soft cushiony bread.

How many times I have wondered at the barefooted glee of that funny girl dancing on a loaf of bread. Of course she got into a lot of trouble with her mom for that pleasureful indiscretion.

She was often getting into trouble for things that were "off limits."

I wrote this poem for her when we took her to see the paper giant, Zozobra, burning in the scary autumn night on a hill in Santa Fe. The myth was that Old Man Gloom, Zozobra, once burned, would end everyone's sorrows.

Hannah was on my shoulders when the huge growling showcase monster was moving his puppet arms and everyone in the field was shouting, "Burn! Burn! Burn!"

Hannah remained stoic. Many children around us were crying and burying their faces in their mother's shirts.

Hannah on the Night Zozobra Burned

Were you scared of Old Man Gloom?
Hannah said, No.
I said, Weren't you scared
he was going to come down the hill
in a roaring rage of sparks?
Hannah said, No.
We went down the arroyo
But before we reached the car,
Hannah said, I pee on Zozobra!

I think of her now as I type this memory. Hannah was not afraid of anything when she was little, nor when she was big, nor now when she raises millions of dollars for nonprofits. She is a fearless fighter but I don't know anyone more gentle.

She and her artist sister are why we are here, back in the high desert again. Yes, there is ock on the mountain, and owls in the elms and Old Man Gloom sleeps in his hundred-foot grave.

Kimball Farms Walker Street
Lenox, Massachusetts (2005)

Some time ago I gave a talk at an assisted living facility and after my storytelling, the friend who had invited me there said there would be a party -- "Just a few people who have known interesting people." I should say so ... one was a Roosevelt, another was the granddaughter of Henry Wadsworth Longfellow, and a third was Winston Churchill's nurse, who said she only smoked cigars with "the old man." As Quarrel says in *Dr. No*, "I like friends that are friends of friends."

A writer I knew was obsessed with Mark Twain. And then one day, while logging a forest in Idaho, the writer met a truck driver, who had known Twain well enough to call him a friend.

Oddly enough, the only time the trucker would talk Twain, as it were, was when he was driving his truck and eating lunch. The trucker was also drinking whiskey. Further, he was disabled--one-armed, one eyed, and he required someone to grab the wheel to negotiate turns because once he started on a Twain recollection he was into his story, his sandwich and his whiskey, and to hell with the road.

But when the harrowing ride was done, my writer friend said he couldn't remember a thing the trucker had said. All he could recall was that the mad truck driving maniac actually had known the great riverman writer. The rest of his recollection was restricted to hairpin turns. Curiously, the writer who met the trucker who knew Mark Twain needed whiskey in order to tell the tale. He told me, "There was the road, the one-eyed, one-armed man and there was Mark Twain. And, you know, I think Sam Clemens ghost was in that truck with us when his name was called, and I think that ghost was urging us off every precipice we came to."

"I guess the ghost of Mark Twain didn't like his name being dropped," I suggested.

"He did like it. That's why he was trying to run us off the road. He wanted to talk to us first hand in the spirit world."

It was my grandfather who said to me, "Shake the hand that shook the hand of one who shook the hand of George Washington." He said that to me when I was twelve in order to let me know that the country, our country was very young. At this same time I remember my father talking about how he met Buffalo Bill at the William Cody Wild West Show at Madison Square Garden in New York City. This must have been around 1904, and coincidentally, Twain was alive then. I asked my dad what Buffalo Bill looked like close up. "When I shook his deerskin gloved hand I looked into his face. But I don't remember that face so much as the silver hair that fell around it. He shined like God's own daydream of a hero."

I loved that gilded age memory and throughout my life I have sought others like it. Once, when I was doing magazine stories about famous people from distant times, I interviewed a Berkshire toymaker who had been friends with Babe Ruth. Sadly, "the Babe" was suffering from "a cancer", as the toymaker said it. "The old home run hitter was sad-faced and fat by then but he loved stalking deer in the woods with his friends, and I was one of them."

He broke off for a moment, deep in thought. Then, he said, "You know, like Thomas Edison who fished without a hook, the Babe hunted with an empty gun. It happens. A man gets older and wiser as time goes by, and he figures out that taking a life doesn't take any courage or forethought, it comes kind of easy to some, but to the old ones, it gets harder and harder to do. I don't kill an ant unless I have to."

Sometimes I wonder what collective memory is, and what, if anything, all these recollections of people in the act of historical remembrance is worth. Sometimes before I go to sleep at night, I say in the voice of the writer who quoted the trucker who knew Mark Twain, "It's been a good life, I've learned a lot, and none of it amounted to very much." And then I compare that statement with my father's: "When I met Buffalo Bill at age four, I heard many people say his name and all said it as softly as a muffled hoof beat on the sawdust of a summer night."

And then I drift off to sleep dreaming of liars, losers, winners and sinners and, as the master said, saintly deceivers.

Old Taos Highway
Santa Fe, New Mexico (1993)

Roger Zelazny was an undisputed master of the long and the short sentence. Here's one of his short ones ...

Such

is

the

kingdom

of

ice

of

ice

such

is

the

And there it ends, frozen. No way to beat that sentence for sound and sense, implication and verification. It's what it is, just as ice is what it is. A long, linear line of coldness, it catches you in its iciness, and makes you wonder. The line comes from *To Spin Is Miracle Cat*.

My other favorite a scroll of wondrous imagery that plays out before the eye in a dazzle of prose poetry:

" ... Places of foundation, where dark streams through darkness flow, blind fish borne through caverns measureless, walls fungus-bright, delineating face and form of all the ancestors of all the tribes of the world, delicate fronds splayed amid coalsheet, beaver, deer, father to himself the bear, the cats, the fish people, bird he had dreamed lifetime but moments before, snake, bat, raccoon, wolf, coyote, and all the insect-folk, amber-cased, dreaming the dream of Her body amid jewels and lakes of oil, and hot rumble of melted rock flowing forever, deep, deep, and light of underworld about him now, and even man and woman, hairy hunters, wanderers in the earth forever, and the big flowers, the strange, unknown flowers, him padding by, blood upon his muzzle, in his mouth his throat, and throws back his head and roars that the underworld know that yet he moves, that nothing has stayed his course since the very beginning."

The above unbroken single sentence comes from the novel that Roger wrote with me, *Wilderness,* the story of mountain man John Colter and hunter Hugh Glass. One man, Colter, runs across the western landscape chased by the best runners of the Blackfeet nation. The other, Glass, crawls after being eviscerated by a grizzly bear and buried alive by his fellow hunters. Colter's naked but for a loincloth, and it is winter. Glass doesn't have the weather against him, but he's got a torn-open belly and he is more "thing" than man.

Curious info on the Master -- Roger used to select his dessert with me in a restaurant before he ordered his meal. Why? Because he always wanted to be sure he had room for that dessert. When he opted to write *Wilderness* with me, I imagine he saw the illuminated book in his mind before he began writing a single word. Some of that scroll above must've flashed before the screen of his consciousness before he said yes to me. It took him a year or more before he put the menu down and ordered the whole book, and at one time, he actually considered "buying the idea" from me. I would've said no. But before he asked me that question I gave him the first chapter. I remember him saying, "This is good. This is very good." The menu was put away.

We worked together. And each morning he brought my wife Lorry a scone.

To tie this all together -- you must dream first, you must spin like miracle cat, you must have the mind of winter to write about ice. You must walk softly and carry a scone. You must write as if it were your first and last sentence.

*

Some readers have recognized the similarity between the novel I wrote with Roger Zelazny, *Wilderness*, and the film with Leonardo DiCaprio, *The Revenant*.

Wilderness was begun in the late 1980s and published by Tor Books in 1994. Roger and I wrote it rapidly but not before doing extensive research on the two men, John Colter and Hugh Glass, who are the main characters of the novel.

I have not read the novel *The Revenant* but film rights were purchased when this book was merely in an unpublished final draft and our novel had been out for a number of years, was widely reviewed and translated into a number of foreign languages. All of which is to say, we were first to present this unusual storyline about two famous mountain men in the wild lands of north America during the 19th century.

A couple readers have told me that it seems that Hugh Glass and Colter were fused into the one character of Hugh Glass in the film. Maybe so, I don't know. What I do know is that there are more than a couple of coincidences in all of this.

In our novel Colter and Glass are fused into one sort of superman-mountain man. Our original title was Colterglass. Our editor at TOR changed it to *Wilderness*.

We wrote about John Colter as an old weary backwoods traveler turned unsuccessful farmer in Missouri; this was at the end of our novel. I'd researched the possibility of Colter, in his final years, meeting up with Hugh in his young years and though the dates were sketchy there was some written proof that this meeting took place at one of the mountain men meeting houses.

By then Colter had aged considerably. He may have been in forties but he looked much older as a result of the privations he endured running 150 miles from the Blackfeet warriors who were pledged to run him down and kill him.

So here we are in an alehouse sometime around 1812. Colter was famous, Glass was a kid yearning to make his mark in the wilderness. The ale house was the yearly meeting place for veteran mountain men. Colter though was weary of "talking tall" as they called it. He settles himself in a corner of the room and listened to the braggarts.

Hugh Glass, the kid, buys Colter, the old guy, a glass of ale. One was about all Colter could handle. Colter tells him:

"If you've a head on your shoulders you'll keep it where it belongs. My advice is to stay in St Louis where you belong."

"I've a mind," Hugh Glass answers, "to see what's back of beyond. Head or no head, I got to see it for myself. Take my chances, sir, just like you." Colter looks the kid up and down and finally says, "I believe you'll outcrawl the likes of me."

A year later Colter was dead of jaundice.

It was Roger Zelazny's contention, while we worked on the novel, that Hugh, having been mauled by a bear, got some of the bear blood in him and became what, as I say above a superman-mountain man. Colter, the same: he crawled through beaver dams and up raw rock in what would become Yellowstone.

Colter crawled when he could no longer run; Glass crawled after the bear mauling and then walked with a limp. The running Glass did was mostly in his mind because that evisceration by the bear was no small thing and most mountain men of that time carried their sundry arrow wounds and bear batterings to the grave.

Both men in the end became legends.

Roger wrote the last page of our book:

Walking then away from it all

down endless caverns,

through citied futures,

one finds, as at the end of every trail,

a skull. Whose is hardly important,

but that into the coming together place

where time crosses the world,

it held the act of continual passion,

granting meaning to the bright moment

of its execution, beneath sun, sky, stars,

where lives and futures fuse ...

It is my contention that the skull, the trail marker, is our book *Wilderness*, originally called *Colterglass*, fusing two brave American heroes into one.

12699 Cristi Way
Pine Island, Florida (2000)

Not everybody *has* to do it...

Not everybody *can* do it...

Not everybody *should* do it...

But the ones who are really good at it, do it every day, and it's like Roger Zelazny said, "You get good at this after a while."

Not necessary to define what it is, or what it isn't, for, as N. Scott Momaday once said, "I'm not a novelist, more of a paragraphist."

"Affix the seat of the pants to the seat of the chair" --Dr Keith Huntress quoting somebody, probably Dr Johnson. Good rule though. Still, you *could* stand and write like Hemingway did.

It's critical for the reader to turn the page. Somewhere or other, *Elements of the Novel*, I think, E.M. Forster says that good storytelling goes back to cave times when around the fire men did sit and boast of the hunt and the bravery & Co., and someone told a foreshortened tale, and someone asked that most pivotal of questions -- "...and then what happened?"

So if the reader doesn't ask that question at the end of each page, the deal's off.

As for style, there's one rule, says William Saroyan --"... write in a manner that implies that death is inevitable ...write in a manner that implies that death is *not* inevitable." Huh?

Of course it's possible to write in a manner that suggests that both life and death are natural and inevitable, but that, given certain circumstances, one or the other is not desirable. One might also say -- leave the door open on that, and let the characters tell you what's up.

Style again...Jack Kerouac had it right when he said it was a matter of breathing, breath units, how you talk is how you write. Talk it out.

Write what you say and how you say it.

"More writers fail from poor character than from poor writing." The poet David Kherdian said that; he also said that, as for fashion, "Writing only goes out so it can come back in."

Best rule of all -- "Being human, you lose it. You can get it back if you know what it is."

Which brings up the last rule.

Keep a notebook with you at all times and ignore those who say, "Scribble, scribble, eh, Mr. Gibbon?"

OK, there's still one more, and maybe this one's really the last. It's about what Roger said, "You get good at this after a while."

"Then why does it get harder?" I asked.

"Because you're getting better."

Finis.

Oh, no. One more.

Never say "finis" at the end of a piece of writing.

12699 Cristi Way
Pine Island, Florida (2010)

The islands, O, Lord, the near and distant ringing loaves of rock burned to carbon, salt and silt, the fringes of mangrove, and the green-gold eyes of panthers and the dark eyes of wide-hipped women given us by Paul Gauguin. The haunted, hunted eyes of Edgar Allen Poe, that dark miscreant of words, inventor of early gothic fictions, that raven-eyed man, so far from the gorgons of Gahan Wilson, but so near to the heart of darkness, so close to Conrad, so far from McMurtry's doves in the desert winds of the Southwest or the hanged woman's ghost in Jane Lindskold's Las Vegas.

And Saroyan, both father and son, O, Lord, so shall we heap praises for the bringing forth of their art in two generations. And many bows to the caverns of the Dordogne, the fluid lines on walls of stone inscribed with butterfly-halved hooves of beasts and seraphic syllables echoed in the caves of the Four Corners, and praises for the yucca-woven sandals of Navajo tribesmen who told what they knew in chants and chafed stone and signatures of petroglyphic art.

Let us bow among the watery ruins of Atlantean landmarks fashioned by Jules Verne and the interstitial spaces where the chronicles of Mars lie perfumed in dust thanks to Ray Bradbury and the roses of Ecclesiastes of Roger Zelazny, and the coyote trunk bait of Trent Zelazny.

Now drop us off at Old Man Pritchard's porch where the boy, Jimmy Nightshade of 97 Oak street is 13 years, eleven months, and 23 days old, and the summer leaves of Green Town, Illinois, now brown and sere on a lonesome night in October where in another part of the world, London, Jack the Ripper is fogged and dogged by his storytelling canine, Snuff.

Shall we follow the footpaths of Mary Shelley, Bram Stoker, A.C. Doyle, H.P. Lovecraft, Ray Bradbury, Robert Bloch, Robert Payson

Terhune, Villiers de L'Isle Adam, Djuna Barnes? Shall we read in the violet shadows, the mist-encrypted figures pass, but never be forgotten, let it all pass but not be forgot, even if it should be but one word of holy writ, one poem, one shard of splintered light from one Leonard Cohen, Wilfred Owen, Edna St. Vincent Millay, Ursula K. Le Guin.

Books to read before you Die

The Moon and Sixpence by Somerset Maugham

Poe: A Life Cut Short by Peter Ackroyd

Books by Larry McMurtry

Leaving Cheyenne by Larry McMurtry

Child of a Rainless Year by Jane Lindskold

The Daring Young Man on the Flying Trapeze by William Saroyan

The Street by Aram Saroyan

Places of Mystery, Power and Energy by Bill Worrell

Twenty Thousand Leagues Under The Sea by Jules Verne

The Greater Journey by David McCullough

1913 by Florian Illies

The Education of Henry Adams by Henry Adams

Eye Of Cat by Roger Zelazny

Rose for Ecclesiastes by Roger Zelazny

A Night in the Lonesome October by Roger Zelazny

The Day The Leash Gave Way by Trent Zelazny

Frankenstein by Mary Shelley

Dandelion Wine by Ray Bradbury

Nightwood by Djuna Barnes

Poems and Songs by Leonard Cohen

Collected Poems by Edna St. Vincent Millay

The Seashell Anthology by Christopher Burns

The Wind's Twelve Quarters by Ursula K. Le Guin

542 Franklin Avenue
Santa Fe, New Mexico (2018)

Some people lend a helping hand. Others bless bumblebees. Fred Rogers did both, and so much more.

I knew Fred Rogers, first of all, as the leading member of a board of directors for the publishing company where I worked as a printing salesman, bookseller, editor, and ghost writer.

One day, inspired by a recent visit from Fred, I wrote a poem entitled "Anyone Can Be A Poet". It was the sort of sentiment I thought Fred would like, praising the mindfulness of the spoken word in the mouths of individuals who never once dreamed of writing a poem, but in a certain sense, lived them every day and spoke them.

Fred was himself, an everyday, anyone poet, who said things that needed to be remembered by others. I guess it's best to say that such poets are oral ones. They don't require the written word to make their message any truer or more honestly real.

Anyway Fred loved that poem and told me so. And he encouraged me to keep writing off-the-cuff in that same way. So I did. And I still do, thanks to Fred.

Years later when HarperCollins published my children's book *Eagle Boy*, I sent it to Fred and he phoned me immediately and said the book was charming and he loved the message about the little boy floating down to earth with bumblebees under his moccasins. When he touches the earth, his mother is waiting for him, and the story ends there with the boy becoming, many years later, a great medicine man.

Fred said, "I praise you for writing this story and doing it well, but even more so for the effort of *wanting* to write it in the first place."

He pointed out that the same desire, that wanting to express something inexpressible, was in the boy as well.

"Do you remember the juniper trees?" Fred asked.

I hesitated for a moment. "Which ones?"

"I am thinking of the ones you put over your upstairs windows in the house you built in Tesuque, New Mexico. You could have just hung curtains. Instead you cut beautiful juniper boughs to shade you from the sun."

"Is that a story I should write?" I asked.

"If you wish to do so. Remember, *anyone can be a poet*," he said.

Then he changed the subject. "Well," he said, "how is that pond of yours?"

I said, "I swim in it every day."

Fred chuckled. "I must come and join you. Soon."

A few months later he was gone and though we had gone swimming together in Pittsburgh, I knew we would never do laps in the little pond next to our house. He had said, "One day we will do that long swim together."

I had remarked, "With bumblebees under our feet."

Now, all these years later, when I look at the long row of children's books in our bedroom, I realize that Fred blessed every one of them with bumblebee pollen.

The Windsor Mountain School
Lenox, Massachusetts (1968);
Santa Fe Preparatory
Santa Fe, New Mexico (1986)

I began writing letters to Philip Whalen when he was in Kyoto in 1968. He wrote me back in the prettiest calligraphy I had ever seen. I thought, if this great poet will write me back more than once I will somehow manage to practice his lovely kind of print/script.

So we began writing to each other. He seemed willing enough but to me every Air Avion folded blue envelope from Japan was a treasure to behold as well as to read. I began my calligraphy lessons with an Osmiroid pen.

I didn't know it then but Phil explained to me later that he had learned the unusual calligraphic style from Reed professor, Lloyd Reynolds. He told me that Gary Snyder had learned to do it too. They were roommates.

And now I was learning. It seemed natural to me, as my mother was a calligrapher whose style was from the 1920s when formal letters in fine handwriting were not only normal but practical.

Back and forth Phil and I corresponded. I asked him all sorts of questions and he answered them. One time I remember that I asked him why he was so good about writing me back so quickly. He returned this: "I wouldn't write you if you were no good."

I loved that. It made me feel good.

Later, in another letter, I asked what magazines I should be sending my poetry to and he responded: Any of them except ones where Eunice Bilkington Fazzbazz is the featured poet."

He just kept giving this down to earth advice, always with a twist of humor. I mentioned in a letter that my friends appeared to be ignorant of my worth as a writer. He wrote back, "When you win the Pulitzer, the Nobel and the American Book Award all on the same day, your friends will be out to lunch and will miss the broadcast of your achievement."

In retrospect, I was a very young poet and he was a legendary Beat writer, best friend of Jack Kerouac, widely anthologized poet. And yet he stuck by me, gave me a blurb for my first book and said he liked my poetry for its "image/experience/flash."

He particularly liked a poem I wrote called "Frog Creek Boulder". What was it he liked about that poem, I asked in another letter. He said, "The candles on the ledges of the falls with the water pouring down."

I began to understand, he liked anomalies. Tensions. Usually ones that were unresolved. Unresolvable tensions of the human condition. He worked at his own resistance by laughing at himself. By seeing that he was destined to trip smack on his face on a delivery of a flower. (That, one of his most famous poems, but it was real, not made up or fantasized.)

And I began to believe that he didn't mind that I was learning, just learning mind you to write in calligraphy.

In the years after Phil left Kyoto, we continued to write to each other. I saw him in San Francisco and Santa Fe when he was a Zen prefect at the zendo in town.

I always wondered how anyone could be truly humble, unconscious of himself and yet so keen of eye as to miss nothing.

I taught his poetry at Santa Fe Preparatory where I was an English teacher the same impassioned way that I used his poetry at The Windsor Mountain School when I was a teacher there. My students seemed to love Whalen's writing because of the humor and the crisp, clear Zen imagery. He was the real thing. So were my students.

One time when I saw Phil at the Zen Center in San Francisco, he said goodbye to me after we'd spent the afternoon together, and as I started to leave, I heard him whisper, "Say hello to Lewis Warsh while you're out there."

Lewis was a poet who was known to me. But I didn't know him. Nor was I planning to. That afternoon while waiting for a bus in Berkeley, I spotted Lewis Warsh standing next to me. I laughed and said, "Phil told me to say hello." Warsh laughed and shook his head. He knew, too, didn't he. We were all a bit 1970s whacked, Zen heroes

of our wild imaginations. Phil, on the other hand, was psychic. But I
never heard him mention the word.

Temporarily Phil

I stuffed Phil's pockets
with tens and twenties once
money my students
gave to me to give to him
after he read
"Sourdough Mountain Lookout"
later we ate lunch
Phil's white shirt
covered with red chile spots
"Seems I can't eat without
getting it on myself"
he said mopping his plate
with a sopapilla
Phil said Jack said,
"One day we'll all be old
railroad bums
together under the bridge
drinking bottles of Tokay wine."
I told him
La Llorona
lived under the bridge.
"Who's that?"
"The woman with no face."
"Ah," Phil said, squinting
"That building over there
is either a publisher or
a whorehouse, so many people
coming and going."
"My publisher," I said.
He laughed, "Good for you."

When I dropped him off
at the zendo we hugged.
I asked when I'd see him again
"You know
I'm only here …"
Sun gleam on blue sage
"… temporarily."

People & Places

The Windsor Mountain School
Lenox, Massachusetts (1968)

I remember the night in 1968 when Richard Nixon was elected president.

I was having Viennese coffee with Gertrud Bondy, who with her husband Max was founder of The Windsor Mountain School where I had just been hired as a teacher.

Gertrud turned to me and said, "I saw Adolf Hitler on the street in Munich during the Beer Hall Putsch of 1923. It was one of those times, like tonight, when you did not know what was going to happen. But you felt the world was soon to change . . . for the worse."

Gertrud had a right to mention Hitler; her life spanned more than eight decades, she had been a student of Sigmund Freud, and later, Carl Jung and her nightmare with the Nazis was a story I would hear many times, and never forget.

She had been close enough to touch Hitler as he strutted down that crowded street. Later, when there was no place left in Germany to run a progressive school, Gertrud and her husband Max brought their students with them to Switzerland in 1937, then to Vermont, and finally, Lenox, Massachusetts where we were on the night of Nixon's election.

"We had a very close call with Hermann Goering," Gertrud continued. "His daughter was in our school in Germany. Goering personally threatened Max's life. "But I never thought any of this could ever happen again."

"Is it?" I asked.

Gertrud's hands were trembling, and it wasn't the coffee. "Nixon will be terrible for this country," she said. "There is no telling what may happen. He is a dangerous man."

A year later, the world was still turning, but as a second-year teacher

I was earning just over 5,000 dollars. In the summer of 1971 our eldest daughter was born, and I was promised a significant raise.

Then, all at once, Nixon was touting an economic move that involved a thing called the Wage and Price Freeze. This was supposed to stop out of control inflation and set the country's shaky economy on the right track.

On August 15, 1971, salaries and prices were frozen. My raise, never a bird in hand, flew off into the ether.

In 1972, things weren't much better. We could barely afford to live. But we were getting good at living on the cheap, living with low expectations, not spending any money, finding new ways to earn money in addition to teaching. This was the beginning of a life-long cycle of teaching full time with three jobs on the side.

During the next five years there was one financial crisis after another, including a major gas crisis which crippled the economy so that staying at home made more sense than going to work. If you couldn't get gas, you couldn't drive. If you couldn't drive, you couldn't make a living.

Looking back now, it was rough going all along the watchtower, as far back as I can remember. But no memory stands out like that night with Gertrud. The way her delicate, gold-rimmed Viennese coffee cup rattled in its saucer as the night horrors of that election rolled in, one frightful state at a time.

Gertrud has been gone a long time but I wonder what she would say about the way things are now.

I can hear her coffee cup rattle as more dangerous men step up to the podium.

Arnoldia
West Brattleboro, Vermont (1970-2018)

Bob and Susan Arnold have been friends with Lorry and me since the start. They are the founders of the oldest continually operating alternative publisher in the U.S. Bob is a wonderful poet whose work in words, like his work in wood, has been consistent beyond measure.

He writes poems and builds houses on his deep-woods acreage in the hills outside of Brattleboro. He also makes free-standing rock walls that look exactly like the pen and ink illustrations of Robert Frost's *Mending Wall*. The walls may lean but Bob's poems do not lean, and that is the only difference.

Come to think of it, maybe his rock walls do lean a little – on purpose -- to follow the curve of the hill.

His poems do that, too. They follow the curve of the landscape of backwoods Vermont.

What Bob and Susan did for me was a lean of a different kind. They published my poems.

Back in the days when alternative meant just that. "Alter-native."

I was an alter-native, and so was Bob.

He was gifted a mimeograph machine by a minister who saw that Bob would do more with it than he could. He did, too. He put out singular, typewritten manuscripts that seemed to have walked out of the woods. Like Bob himself.

Using his Longhouse imprint, he brought out an early draft of a chapter from my first novel, *No Witness*, about UFOs and Navajo werewolves. When I was doing a lot of long distance running in the Southwest, Bob brought out a handmade booklet in my own calligraphic hand called *Anasazi Honey*. Five years ago, Bob told me to gather all the poems I could find and he would put them between covers and call it Selected Poems.

This was 35 years past the days of the minister's mimeograph. A few years ago Lorry and I drove to Arnoldia to see what new cabins Bob had built. The hill where their house sits is one building among many. The entire woods is notched and niched with the prettiest woodland homes. Each one, whether granite stone or hand-hewn log, old style clapboard cottage, or A-frame, is a work of art. Just like Bob's books.

Arnoldia is a place, a place holder, a haven of art, books, and dreams. There is even a blackboard that looks out on the river road so that cars passing by can read the poems Bob posts.

Sometimes the drivers honk, wave, or say something personal. That blackboard means something to the many who see it in passing.

To those who don't, well, Bob has a curious smile that reminds me of friendship, poetry and back road callers. He doesn't mind when people miss something. They'll get it. One day.

Club West
Santa Fe, New Mexico;
Rancho Encantado,
Tesuque, New Mexico (1984)

He turned up at a club in Santa Fe called Club West. He played to a nearly empty house one night, a full one the next, and then he was off again into the thin mountain air.

So it goes with Jack Elliott -- here today, gone tomorrow. Not so with his music. Jack is to folk music what another Jack-of-trades, Kerouac, is to literature. Both of them men of myth, men of magic. No accident they hung around together a half century ago, two, true blue, lonesome travelers. Woody Guthrie, who preceded them in legend, called Jack Elliott, with whom he rambled the country many times over, "the great American legend."

Legends and stories are part of our national fabric. No surprise then that Ramblin' Jack Elliott's name is made up, and the man himself is a patchwork quilt of casual observations, awkward stances, soft twangs and flat picker's nuances all rolled into one man whose identity was once summed by Arlo Guthrie: "We all have the capacity to become nobody, but very few of us have the ability to be everybody or anybody. Jack not only has the ability but the stubborn will to live the lives of all men."

John Greenway, music critic, put it this way: "Trying to get at the true Jack Elliott is like swimming in a bucket of oatmeal."

Johnny Cash once told Jack to watch out for Hollywood and not to let Hollywood rub off on him. "On the other hand, keep rubbing a little of Jack Elliott off on them."

*

I remember being a 17-year-old kid when my friend Jimmy MacFadyen and I rambled over to Greenwich Village where we met our folk hero, Ramblin' Jack in front of the Gaslight Cafe. He had a girl under each arm and each was pretty beyond compare and Jack was not wearing his usual black cowboy hat but instead a small blue seaman's cap, but he looked like a real sailor on horseback -- tight faded jeans and a wide rimmed smile, if not hat, sun-squint creases at the corners of his eyes.

Well, there he was -- a storyteller of our times, in the flesh. The pretty girls had faded away and Jack was left on the sidewalk with two green folksy fools, and now he took us into The Gaslight and treated us to a night of folksongs, always at our request, and it went like that for hours. He didn't seem to care about the rest of the audience, or his lost girlfriends, he just sang to us. Sometimes he even said directly, "What do you boys want to hear now?"

Around 20 years later, with me grown up and with two daughters under my arm, I met Jack again at a party in Tesuque, New Mexico at the ranch house of our friend, Ronnie Egan. My brother Sid, also a folksinger of more than one note (and a friend of Jack's) was there, and so we all sat around and spun some tales, played guitars and then my brother dropped a bomb and told Jack, "Gerry can sing some of your songs, Jack, and he sounds like you, too."

Jack grinned, handed over his Martin D-18.

My fingers were trembling but I got through at least one rendition of "Hobo's Lullaby" and sometimes it even sounded to *me* like Jack was doing it.

His grin stayed lit for that, and for a few others I did, and when I passed his guitar back to him, I realized that Sid had done me a great favor. It was a rite of passage. I might never have to sing like that again but there it was.

What followed was weirder. My eldest daughter, Mariah, who was a teen at the time, asked Jack if *he* could do imitations. That made him laugh, partly because he was the inventor of *chameleonism*, but also because Mariah was so cute the way she asked.

So he did a volley of quick-pick soliloquys -- Matt Dillon, who was very popular at the time, plus some other heroes of the moment, and then Jack picked up his guitar again and did a remembrance of his old busking buddy, Derroll Adams, the banjo picker, when they had wandered along the Seine in the 1950s, and then he was doing an Irish tenor singing in the rigging of a square rigger, and a little Woody Guthrie thing, too.

"There, that satisfy you?"

Mariah smiled and nodded.

A few weeks later Jack called me on the phone. He was in Coney Island then and his father was dying. "I feel close to my own death here with my father sick and going into a rest home."

"What are you going to do back there?"

"Maybe hole up for a while and write down the story of my life. You said you knew someone who'd publish it."

I did, and I thought then of the 14-year-old boy he had been when he ran away from home and joined up with the rodeos, all that mileage and melodic movement across America, all that weaving of his own legend, all that great American bum mythology, all that Big Rock Candy Mountain climbing.

I don't really know if Jack scratched the literary surface of his story on paper. I don't know if he ever wrote his memoir, but I sure would like to read it, wouldn't you? If I were publishing it, I would use Jack Kerouac's lines from his *Book Of Dreams*: "Later it was a long happy dream of the backyard on Phebe Avenue and Jack Elliott the Singin' Cowboy has made a record which is selling a million copies and we're all together in the happy yard."

Tesuque
New Mexico (1987)

In the beginning there was Water Woman, and the world, her world, was calm and still.

So Water Woman made Earth and Sky, who were twins. In time, the twins made Black-Belted Mountain, Turquoise Mountain, Colored-Cloud Mountain and Big Sheep Mountain.

After the mountains were made, there was still no life, such as we know it, so Earth created Black God, who is the god of fire. Then she made Horned Toad, Locust, Blue Lizard, First Man and First Woman, and Ant. There was Red Ant, Yellow Ant, Black Ant and Many-colored Ant, and all of the Ant People had light coming out of them.

Still, there was no life.

Then Earth breathed life into Wind and, in turn, Wind breathed life into all things, and the things of life came alive and lived.

One night, as it happened, the house was full of ants. They swarmed in the sugar bowl on the table and were all over the floor, the ceiling, the walls and they were even in the beds of the house.

My friend Joogii came by on that same day the ants arrived, and as his father was a medicine man, I asked him what his father would do.

"He pushed his black cowboy hat back on his head and asked a question of his own -- "What have you done?"

"Nothing much -- yet."

Joogii smiled. "It is my training that anything you do is of consequence -- even nothing. . . sometimes . . . especially . . . nothing."

"Well, I killed a bunch. "Had to, " I confessed. "No other way."

"There were just so many," my wife Lorry explained. "You couldn't even walk without stepping on them."

Joogii lowered the brim of his hat and it was as if a black-belted horizon had come down level with his eyes. "Whenever you kill something," he offered quietly, "you have to cleanse yourself."

"-- How?"

"The usual way. Burn some cedar in the house."

" --That all?"

Joogii raised the brim of his black-belted hat with his forefinger. Black eyes and nutbrown face gleaming. "Come here," he said. He walked outside, we followed. In a moment or two, Joogii found a tall conical ant hill. We stood there in the sun, the three of us, throwing long blue shadows.

"Let's not let our shadows get ahead of us," Joogii said, amused. He chuckled, then turned a different angle to the sun. His shadow shifted like a dark blade, thinned, disappeared.

Joogii knelt down. I thought he was going to do a chant. But he didn't. We listened as he said in a kind of respectful whisper, "Tell these ants you're sorry you lessened their number. Tell them you're sorry for what you did. Tell them you won't do it again. Tomorrow, go out and find a horned toad; put him right here, by this same hill."

"Is that all?" I asked.

Joogii grinned. "It's enough."

That night I burned the juniper bough in the house filling it with cedary sweetness. I went from room to room with the fragrant, flaming stick and then I put it outside and walked to the ant hill and said I was sorry. In the morning, I found a large sun-dappled horned toad and placed it by the hill and left it there and went about my business, which is the writing of books.

Lorry came to me at noon and said, "You should see. No ants in the sugar bowl."

I looked up from my computer screen. "Any ants in the house?"

"No."

She and I walked outside into the bright New Mexican sun.

We sat on a fallen juniper, and watched.

The horned toad was there. It would arch its back and lift itself up and then it's whole body made a sharp stab at an ant emerging from the hole. It happened too fast to see it, really. The ant was there, and then it wasn't. Obviously, these ants didn't know who Horned Toad was. They didn't know the ancient myth; they didn't know the rule. They tried to come out, they got eaten up. We saw four ants eaten that way, very quickly.

Then -- as we watched the ancient story unfolded.

*

Lone Ant Rider, larger than the others, came forward from the lip of the mound that was the Ant People's home, and he said, "Where are the four Ant People who were just here a moment ago?"

Horned Toad said, "I ate them."

"What did you do that for?" Lone Ant Rider asked.

"I cannot help it," Horned Toad replied.

"Why can you not help eating them?" Lone Ant Rider asked.

"Because it is that way."

"It wasn't always that way."

"Maybe you never noticed," Horned Toad said.

Now there were a great many Ant People who had come up the ant ladder and were now boiling all around, making furious movements of the hands and feet, and they became irritated all of a sudden, and started biting one another. In no time there was an Ant People war.

Lone Ant Rider, knocked off his feet, was being bitten by the jaws of many of his kind. "Is this how it is?" he asked Horned Toad.

Horned Toad said, yes, and Lone Ant Rider was borne away in a river of ant bodies, all of whom were fighting and biting and tearing each other apart.

Horned Toad came near this raging river and spoke to the fighting ants swarming there. "Because you won't behave, I am going to eat all of you. But don't worry -- I will leave enough of you, and some will always remain. That is the way it is."

*

The Ant People were too busy killing each other to hear Horned Toad, and he ate all of them but two -- Ant Man and Ant Woman.

That night, Joogii drove up in the tribal truck with the Navajo flag of the bear that Joogii had created himself for The People; I remembered him doing this when we were young men thirty years before.

Joogii eased himself out of the cab and came into the house and asked me to make him some Sleepytime tea. I set the tea kettle on the gas stove and Joogii asked Lorry if the ants were still around.

"We did what you told us to do," she said.

His eyes asked other questions, but he didn't say anything.

When the tea was ready, I set it before him with some honey and a spoon. Joogii helped himself. "Some time ago," he said, sipping, "Earth grew tired of the ways of the Ant People and so she told Black God, Fire God, to set fire to the corners of the earth. And then all created beings moved to the center where they were pushed to the top of the sacred mountains into the next world where everything was much brighter. Some say there are four worlds --"

"What is the one we're in now?" Lorry asked. She put a plate of cookies on the table.

Joogii munched on a Lorna Doone. Wiping the crumbs from his lip, he said, "Fourth or fifth, depending on who you are, what you think."

"Anyway, the ants are gone," she added pleasantly.

"Not gone," Joogii corrected. "Lessened."

"Each world gets brighter?" I wondered aloud.

"That's what they say."

"Are we . . . the Ant People?"

"No, but we sure as hell fight like them."

That night I placed a marijuana seed at the top of the ant hill. In the morning the green seed was gone. In its place, there was a tiny piece of turquoise.

Blue Harbour
North Coast, Jamaica (1988)

The way this story goes, it sounds like there is only one man in all of Jamaica who has the answers, the remedies of the people, the gift of the golden tongue. Not true.

Almost everyone in Jamaica has a touch of it, some more than others, but all as gifted as the chick-mon-chick bird singing in the forest. Jamaica is a place of mystery, and aside from the poverty that visits so many there, a place of cool runnings, as they say.

Mr. Morris Oliphant is one, but Prof-I is yet another. Prof-I was Peter Tosh's cook. We asked him to come to our school and prepare Jamaican patties, the ital way, the all-natural, no salt added way, and he did.

Our students loved them, and salted them.

There was Horace, better known locally as Winston Churchill, or just plain Churchill.

All three of these guys – Morris, Prof-I and Churchill were natural mystics and made what we might call remedial potions. In New Mexico the special folk medicines are called *Remedios de la Gente.*

In Jamaica such tonics can heal a great many illnesses. But first "You must have that intention," as Countryman says in the film of that name.

The useful potion for curing a cold is a pinch from each of these natural mystics -- some white rum, some little pimento berries, some bush weed marijuana, and for good measure, a bit of scotch bonnet pepper. Scotch bonnet, by the way is considered one of the hottest peppers on the planet.

So you put them in the "bokkle" and let them steep for, let's say, six months. After that one tablespoon can cure a cold. Any cold, so they say. Even cancer, some say. And, after a while, you just take out the Mason jar, put a spoon beside it, and threaten whatever it is you have that is troubling you, and it will quail and go away.

On most nights I walk through the bush to the old abandoned block house where Morris Oliphant sits before a fire of pimento wood.

In Jamaica at night the croaker lizards start up early, calling across the guango trees in the dusk. The peepers chime in four beat rhythms, always the same, over and over, and a man named Morris Oliphant, who is said to know the secrets of life and death, body and soul, waits for me in the darkness.

I come to him hoping that one day he will show me the potion I have heard so much about. The potion is what keeps Mr. Oliphant from growing old. It's like the mysterious hot spring in St Ann that curdles with blue flames on top of the water. It is like the spirit of the Water Moomah who inhabits the springs where we live and the great yellow boa that, according to legend, once got a girl pregnant.

Mr. Morris is a man who never ages; no one knows his real age. He walks and talks in mysterious zones and tones. Some say his family came from Martinique long ago. Some say he dropped from the sky and they laugh when they say it.

I find him sitting on a stone, his machete balanced on his right knee. A small fire is before him and a large breadfruit with blackened skin cooks on the coals.

I take my place on a stone. And wait.

For a while we sit in our own private silence -- mine, his, the fire's, the night's -- and then Mr. Morris speaks in that quiet knowing way of his.

"Give thanks and praises, Gerry mon. For life, not death, for it is life we live. And it is life we know, and death, me no penetrate that yet, nor did anyone come back from that place and tell us about it. So it must remain the great mystery, the next rung in the ladder Jacob must climb."

"They say you know a man that wouldn't die. 'Hard man fi dead', as they say. A man right out of the Bible."

"Why you ask that?"

Behind his head the blinkies, lightning bugs, punctuate the dark.

"I like mysteries," I tell him.

"Yes, mon, that is what I hear."

"I am drawn to any question that hasn't a ready answer."

"All right. True. There is no heaven, no hell except on earth, y'know. It all man-made, just like the Tower of Babel that plunge we into confusion. Once we could talk to animal and thing, bird and bee and man, but no more. So hear me now, there was a man name Samson. Him live inna the bush, like you see me here. This man Samson big and strong like a guango. No man trouble him. During the day him work in the field as a plowman, but at night, once a month, Samson count his shilling and pence by candlelight. Some tief in the village come to tek what is not theirs to have. Them is three against one. And them have a gun. So them shoot Samson in the face. That bullet rip out a rotten molar -- trouble him long time, now it gone. Then them shoot Samson again but him roll pon him stomach. Second bullet catch him in the backside and knock out a sciatic nerve that vex him many a year. So the tief them nuh kill Samson. Him a hard man fi dead. And him smite them good. Y'know what Samson say?"

He pauses. Then looks me in the eye in the firelight.

"Keep no lock on your money, just pon your head. And him live long. No one know how long him live. Him just *live*."

"So, Mr. Morris, it's as you say -- there is *only* life."

He laughs, we touch knuckles. "If you *see* it that way, you *live* it that way. No man fear death who *live* life!"

As I walk back home through the wet banana leaves, there is no light to see. There is nothing but to feel the path under my feet. A false step and I might fall off the cliff. But then I know that I would just climb up back, for, slowly and inexorably, I am being *Samsonized* on this rare, beautiful, genius gem of an island, *Coyaba*, which means "place of ease and rest" in Arawak, or simply, heaven in English.

Red River
New Mexico (1982)

"You know, he said, sipping rum, "I would really like to make love."

"I don't really feel like it right now," she replied with a quick sip.

He dropped two juniper logs into the fireplace.

She was standing almost directly in front of the fire and her figure, hauntingly slim, was shadowed in all the right places and the edges of her body were fire-haloed. This peeved him -- seeing her look so inviting, so delectable and his not being able to get any of it, and most of all, her hair was the same color as the firelight. It made him nervous.

"Move out of the way," he advised, dropping on one more log.

She stepped away, the fire cackled and danced.

Then she sat close to the flames warming her skin.

He sighed loudly, sadly. "Let me lie at your feet," he suggested.

She made a place for him, and he put his head on her thigh and lay back and enjoyed the fire and its tangling light in her hair.

She was beautiful. But more than that, desirable.

"It's not sex, really," he said.

"It's not?"

"Not really.

"What is it then?"

"Closeness. I want that."

She smiled. "I understand."

He felt her relax a little. He felt her thigh grow softer, and she lay back with her head resting on her hands and her hip turned upwards and her legs drawn up.

His head remained where it was and he was warm but the brick floor was cold and he asked, "Is there any more rum?"

She shook her head. "We finished it."

He saw the empty bottle glittering and the two empty glasses.

"Look," he said, "we don't have to have sex."

"We're not going to."

"I know. But maybe we should have a blanket."

"All right."

He raised his head off her thigh and she got up and got an old soft Pendleton blanket.

They sat up, cross-legged, very close with the blanket over their shoulders. He put his arm around her and his hand on her left hip. The firelight played on them prettily and the wind outside uttered a warning and he felt a chill run through him.

She sat perfectly still, as if she were something the fire, the flames had actually sculpted out of clay. Then she broke the pose and stretched, yawned, and while she did so, and was leaning back, a little of her stomach showed whitely and seemingly tickled by the flames, and he reached boldly down and unzipped her jeans and stroked the fine silk of her panties.

"What is that noise outside?"

"Nothing."

"What do you think you're doing?"

"What do you mean what am I doing?"

She looked from the door to the window to his hand.

Then she pulled the blanket around her.

He was outside the blanket, but his hand was under it and it was also right where it was, softly stroking. Soft as the flames. Very gentle. Very light, touch and go, almost abstract.

He unzipped his jeans. He was ready. Too ready. But there was nothing to be done about it except to say, "I just want to lie down on top of you."

"Go ahead," she said.

"You'll have to lie down."

"All right," she said, "but I'm not taking the blanket off."

"I didn't ask you to."

At last, they were horizontal in a vertical world.

He whispered into her ear. "I am just going to lie on top of you."

"All right," she said.

He continued soft-stroking.

"I am just going to pull off your panties."

She did not respond.

He waited. His heart was beating hard.

"All right?" he asked, his fingers on the elastic.

She sighed. "Go ahead."

He drew down her jeans and the panties came halfway with them. Then he smoothly removed the jeans at the hems, pulled them hollowly down off her bare legs and off her feet.

The firelight made prayerful feints and flashes like hands coming together and parting, like soundless clapping, like water lapping soundlessly, and her panties were halfway. He applied fingers and thumbs to them, and drew them away more gently than anything he had ever done. They made no sound, not even a whisper as they slipped along her thighs and were then gone and of no importance.

"I am just going to put myself in ... a little way," he said.

She said nothing. Then, "All right."

He did that thing.

He waited, breathed, listened.

She made no movement but for the slightest shifting of her legs.

"Now I'm going to move three times closer in," he said.

She murmured, "Do."

He did.

Then, as was their way, he began counting.

He got as far as ten and then he could not count any more.

Finally, she held him fast to her and her fingernails became claws.

He lost count of the times he went and he no longer asked anything of her and she gave him everything he wanted without asking and this went on for a good many hours.

And thus, in the morning, she who had refused all others, made Coyote her lover.

Off Bishop's Lodge Road
Santa Fe, New Mexico (1990)

Then back into the warm womb, where, chin on knee, the cedar-branched roof of the sweat lodge holds the heat in. The wrath of hot rocks teased to the cracking point by river water. The Pueblo prayer over and over in the ear.

Larry Littlebird is a small Tewa man, hair down back. I can't quite see him in the dark of the lodge but I can hear him along with the hiss of the stones as he prays and pours more water on them bringing the heat into my nose so that when I try to draw air, it burns. My head lowers in the inescapable heat.

Bow down, then, in the dark.

Bow down to the mother that bore you.

Bow down to mother earth.

Bow down to sky, star and wind.

Bow down to the fire-master and friend who invites you to this bodily purification, and do not forget the words, the prayers, the sweet salt of which the body is made, and the fire of the blood that boils out the sweet salt do not forget.

The roof of cedar touches my head.

My legs are crossed, head bent, back bowed.

Littlebird's voice and the stones speaking in Tewa, the old language of the earth: "We thank the mystery of fire," he says, "the sweet salt that comes freely from our pores, the blood of our hearts, the beauty that is all round us, that is in us, that surrounds us from the top of our heads to the tip of the toes, the air that we breathe, the water that the fish breathe, the hot, the cold, the good, the bad, which, we, Grandfather, in our blindness as in this lodge do not always choose to understand, O, Grandfather, we are blessed, thank you, thank you, thank you, thank you."

Larry's voice fades.

The stones speak.

More scalding steam.

More sweet salt.

The few that remain, naked in the darkness, get up and go. They do not return. The heat has driven them out into the night where the temperature is below zero.

Larry and I, then, alone.

He clacks the deer antlers and the small molten moths leap up from the embers and fly in front of my eyes. He throws sage on the red-hot stones and instantly the high mesa is all round, sweet fragrance of a summer night. "Now, you say what you are thankful for," Larry says to me.

I do not hesitate: "For the smoke of cedar and the elder watching over us for our nakedness and our being alive for waking, walking, wondering, wanting, working, seeing for the hours and prayers, Grandfather, thank you, thank you, thank you, thank you."

Laughing in the darkness, Larry asks, "Did you forget something?"

" -- What?"

Larry opens the blanket flap of the lodge revealing the night of frosted stars. "You forgot to thank Grandfather for the plunge in the ice-cold stream that follows the sweat."

Then Larry gets up quickly like a man going to catch a ride somewhere. After which he walks slowly and deliberately into the river, rubbing the ice water on his skin.

I follow and do the same.

And the flakes come tumbling down and whiten our heads before our time and Larry says, "We're just here for a while" but whether he means the river, or something deeper, I don't know and he doesn't explain.

12699 Cristi Way
Bokeelia, Florida (2008)

I was editing *The Image Taker* for World Wisdom Publishing. This was a book featuring the collected writings and photographs of Edward S. Curtis. The first editions of the book had appeared in foreign languages and had gotten a fair amount of press. But in re-working it for World Wisdom I found myself tripping over the name Two Guns White Calf, one of the most iconic native people I'd ever seen. I didn't realize at the time that one of my very best friends had met Two Guns.

My ninety-five-year-old friend, Karl asked me if I knew what a Buffalo Nickel looked like.

"Of course I do," I told him, "and the buttons on my black dress shirt testify to this, all nickel-bright buffaloes and Indians."

Karl smiled. "Well, all right, so you know ... but did you know that I met the man on the coin on 57th Street in New York City when I was just a little boy?"

I asked, "Did I ever tell you that my dad met Buffalo Bill Cody on 42nd Street in New York City when he was a little boy?"

"Buffalo Bill's Wild West Show?"

"Just so."

"Well," Karl said, "The buffalo, I mean the bison, as the school teachers would have us say today, is on one side of that classic coin and on the flipside is Two Guns White Calf who signed his name pictographically: calf and gun."

A month to the day later I was on Useppa Island off the Gulf side of Florida at a little museum. And right there on the wall was a life-size portrait of Two Guns standing there in full regalia, as we used to put it, and next to Two Guns was his friend, Mary Roberts Rinehart, the great 1930s author of American mystery novels.

I could not get close enough to Two Guns. I kept getting closer and closer though until our noses nearly touched. "I meet you at last," I said, and then, "Karl sends his regards."

Sadly, two years later my friend Karl was gone to his own nickel-studded reward, his own happy hunting ground and I learned that our hero Two Guns, the son of a Blackfeet chief, "The handsomest man alive," as Karl had said to me, was not who he was supposed to be. Or was he?

Truth is tricky and truth be known, it turns out that Two Guns' face might not be on that celebrated coin originally designed in 1913 by James Earl Fraser. History seems to falter, or fall away into myth on this silver-sided issue. Karl would not be pleased to know that Fraser himself said the model might be Two Moon, a Cheyenne man. Or, maybe, just maybe Two Guns, or possibly another Indian altogether.

Rodeo cowboy Jimmy Rogers, who as a boy grew up in Colonel Eskew's Wild West Show and also rode with Roy Rogers, said the distinguished face on the coin belonged to Iron Tail, a Lakota Sioux. How did he know? "Well," he said, "I *knew* Iron Tail."

I wonder why I am wondering about all these disparate things. Here I am in a trailer in Questa, New Mexico, mid-spring in a mild snowstorm of high mountain flakes. I pull the covers up to my chin, and dream. And wake to the boom of a high caliber gun. And then another of the same. I jump out of bed and shout, "Two Guns? Forgive me … I never doubted it was you!"

Watergate Hotel and The Kennedy Center
Washington, DC (2005)

In 2005 I was asked by the Kennedy Center to read from my book *The Boy From Nine Miles: The Early Life Of Bob Marley* with my co-author Cedella Marley. We were to meet at The Watergate Hotel in Washington DC and proceed from there.

Our plane was late leaving and early arriving. There we were in the Watergate, which was weird enough, but the elevator insisted on taking us to the top floor where the man pulled the lever and said, "You want to meet the ghost of Richard Nixon? He skulks around on this floor."

I looked at the elevator man. He was tall, dark and oddly tattooed with a scar that ran down the full right side of his face. He grinned and said at the open door, "I am from Liberia and I know what it means to have bad rulers. That's how I got this scar you are looking at. Seeing Nixon's ghost is another thing." He laughed.

It was four in the morning and the face of Nixon, the very idea of the man, haunted us. And as it turned out our room for the night was directly across the way from the long ago office of Daniel Ellsberg. That haunted us too.

I went to bed thinking about those crazy days in 1973 and the black and white TV given to us by a friend who insisted we should see what was going on in Washington. Prior to then we had no television. We were what was called "Dropouts" – not hippies but flipped-out dippies who dipped in and out of the woodlands of the Berkshires, writing poetry and staying out of the mainstream where the world was so ablaze in political chicanery.

Lying in bed at the Watergate I thought those scary times. The headmistress of the school where I taught poetry had been in Germany during the rise of Hitler and she had once stood only a few feet away from him. Her husband's life had been threatened by Hermann Goring who had held a luger to his skull.

I thought about those times and the days of the Nixon impeachment and then I remembered when I was five and my father pointed out a neighbor of ours in Maryland. The neighbor was Whittaker Chambers, the former editor of *Time*. Chambers had been ruined by an ambitious young attorney named Richard Nixon.

I thought about all these things and the elevator man from Liberia who told us that the price of freedom was a facial scar that ran from his forehead to his chin. In Jamaica they called that a "telephone scar" and it was given to people who talked too much.

The following day we, Cedella and I, read from our book about her father and how as a boy little Bob Marley was kidnapped from the tiny St. Ann village, Nine Mile, by his father and taken to Kingston where for one year he disappeared, and his mother could not find him.

At the end of that day I could still hear the applause of the audience that liked our reading. My mind was aflame with names – Bob Marley, the Jamaican revolutionary, Whittaker Chambers, the fallen communist, Hitler, Göring, Ellsberg and Nixon. None of them related except in the history books, all of them dead and buried.

That is when I began feel that the Liberian elevator man was a true hero. Unknown in any history book but still alive. I wrote a poem in his honor and put it in the pocket over my heart.

12699 Cristi Way
Pine Island, Florida (August 9, 2004)

Hurricane Charley supplied me with a lot of ink and even a Best Column Award for "Rose" -- but more than anything else, Charley gave me a sense of courage. We stayed home for a category five with all of our animals -- Great Danes, Siamese cat, European Shorthair, Blue-Fronted Amazon Parrot, Dachshund and a host of unseen geckoes and Cuban tree frogs. Seems like Charley and the animals taught us more than we can ever repay: thanks to each and all.

The day Charley churned across Pine Island Sound and did a mad, destructive dance in Bokeelia, we were in our kitchen expecting the worst. From between the storm shutters, we peeked at the wind-whipped froth that sent bass from our pond hurtling through the air. Wingless bass flying through wind-bent, earth-pressed paperwood trees. No dream of life ever seemed more surreal. However, when Charley tired of sawing up slash pines, there came a dripping, dew-bright moment that was the eye of calm, the eye of false peace. Then after the ripping and the raging continued for a while, Charley seemed to get bored with woods wrecking and roof-pulling, and he spiraled out across Indian Field and then into Charlotte Harbor, whence he made his way, as everybody knows, to Punta Gorda.

We came out of our bolthole, blinking at the new world that lay before us.

It was indeed a brave new world, for which the phrase "wrath of Charley" has no significance. Mainly because it doesn't describe the haunted, unleaved, and in many cases, bare-barked trees. Or the canopies of vines woven into a tornadic tapestry that swung dreamily from the broken stalks of pines and palms.

A new world, yes. A wet and gleaming world that bore no resemblance to the Garden of Eden we'd shuttered off just two hours before when we locked and bolted ourselves into our house.

Miraculously the house still stood.

But it had taken a battering. Lorry and I, after counting our blessings, fell to that other preoccupation--counting our losses. This began with tropical trees, hand-planted so many years ago, to such things as shingles, soffit and fascia. The pool enclosure, so much a part of the house itself, was gone, much of it blown into our pond at the same time the bass were blowing out, most likely.

Anyway, it looked incongruous out there, like the spars of a black ship rising from the gloom of the green swamp.

I looked all around; nothing seemed familiar. Everywhere, rising from the plangent earth in ghosts of steam was the burnt, bruised fragrance of ripped roots and crushed leaves.

At last my eye fell on something known, something dear. A scraggly little rose bush that lived by our lanai. Its bony back was neither bent nor broken, and, unaccountably, there was one bright red-orange rose popping out among the purplish leaves.

"Hey," I cried out to Lorry, "here's a little guy unbeaten by Uncle Charley."

We stooped to admire the hardy little bush. Its brittle bark had been stripped clean of the lichen crusts that we'd been too busy to scrape off all summer.

In reverence, I touched the blossom, and it toppled lazily onto the ground. There was a sad second where I stared in disbelief. Then, turning away from sadness, I fetched the flower, and with a smile of hope, gave it to my wife.

She christened the flower, Hope, and put it in a crystal shot glass filled with water. And so we went about our lives that day, readying ourselves for the great indoor camping trip that would begin and end in our own house two weeks later.

During the day, however, I often spoke of the rose. How Charley had brought it forth. So, from destruction, creation. From bombs bursting to buds breaking. In *The Bhagavad-Gita*, the classic mystical work of ancient India there are these words of rapture that express what I was feeling.

You are the gods of wind,
death, fire, and water;
the moon; the lord of life;
and the great ancestor,
homage to you,
a thousand times homage!
I bow in homage to you
again and yet again.

That evening another miracle occurred: the phone rang.

The power had been out since Charley's blue eye had gazed on Bokeelia. We were without power and water. In addition, the phone line—pinned down by fallen pines—was lying on the ground.

Therefore, we jumped when the phone rang.

I approached the receiver as I had the rose—gently. The sound as I pressed it to my ear was that of a hollow shell at the beach. A kind of *OM*. Then I heard the bright yet distant voice of Kelvin, our horticulturist friend from Trinidad.

No one knew the dark demon *Hurucan* better than Kelvin.

The first thing I said to him was, "How did you do that?"

"How did I do what?" he asked.

"Call us."

He laughed, then said, "I heard you were having a hurricane."

That seemed to say it all. Still, I was astounded.

"You got through," I murmured.

"Yes, mon," he assured me.

"How? Our phone's been dead."

"Love always gets through," he replied, as unsurprised by the munificence of his answer as I was overwhelmed by its beauty.

We went on, then, to talk about what had happened. How Charley had been a very bad boy. How our house had held up. How so many others had not. Kelvin was the perfect person to talk to after living through a category four. He'd been through a hundred tropical storms and who-knows-how many hurricanes. He was so reassuring, so respectful and yet amused, so endearing, so wonderful that I forgot the seriousness of what we were up against—the grim aftermath, the insurance woes, the broken parts of our home.

I didn't say a word about those things, though. Instead, I told Kelvin about the rose that bloomed in the midst of Charley's winds.

"Are there no more blossoms on it now?" he wondered.

"She gave us all she had, I think."

"No," Kelvin said, laughing. "You must go out there and tell that brave rose bush how much you love her, and how many more flowers you want to see her make."

"You mean that?"

Kelvin's laugh, because it's so deep and genuine, is infectious. I was laughing, too—for the first time since Charley. "Listen, my friend," Kelvin said, finally growing serious, "tell that *rose* how much you love her. Tell her, and she'll give you more blossoms."

"Is that how you do it in Trinidad?" I asked.

"We're in short supply of Miracle Grow, my brother. But there's no shortage of love here. There's lots of love in the things of this world."

"So you want me to speak to a rose bush."

"Yes, mon. "Tell her," he continued, "how brave she was facing that wind all by herself. Tell her—well, tell her whatever you want but let it come from the heart."

And with that, the phone went *zzzttt*, and then went dead.

In honor of our long-term friendship and Kelvin's infallible wisdom when it comes to the things of this world, I went directly outside into our ruined garden, and did what he'd told me to do.

As I stood in the ruined garden uttering praises, a heron flew over the pond. A warm glow flowed through me. I felt so grateful for being alive. And somehow, even after Charley, I was still in love with Pine Island. It seemed at that moment, the most enduring place on earth.

The following day, we started to clean up.

However, by day's grueling end, my wife and I were fumbling, tired, and hot. It was 92 degrees in the shade. We were both staggering and the dog fence—so necessary in our yard with the Great Danes—was far from finished. I told Lorry, "I'm going inside to call the fence guy."

She said, "With what phone? You know the line's dead."

I sighed, and looked to the sky. It seemed like it was going rain.

"Hey," she said, "We can do this."

Then two red-shouldered hawks settled in a broken-off pine tree a few feet from us. They bobbed their heads, as if sighting something. Then they froze and gave us a red-eyed, sharp-beaked stare that went into our hearts. After which, in two divergent yet equally strident shrieks, the hawks screamed at us. Maybe they were sounding off about the dismal, dark state of the world, but at that moment, I didn't think so.

To me, it seemed, the hawks were talking to us.

And, out of respect, we listened.

They were such beautiful birds, a matched pair. Their shoulders were rusty-patched, each with a dark tail that had white bands on it. I'd never been this close to a red-shouldered hawk. After eyeing us and scolding us, both birds flew off, leaving the pine branch twanging behind them. Up into the Charley-polished air, the two hawks soared, and then, seemingly to underscore their message, they made a sharp and sudden descent, aimed in our direction. Each hawk fell in a series of perfectly turned, upside-down pirouettes. One roll after another, until, heading right for us, they broke off, singing that high song of angry triumph and crying despair.

I wiped the sweat from my eyes. Saying nothing, my wife and I finished fixing the fence. After seeing the hawks, we found silence more comforting than words. We just worked quietly and uncomplainingly until we were done. The fence, after we were finished with it, looked pretty good. Would it stand up to a galumphing Great Dane? We didn't care. But as we were walking back to the house with our tools, I said, "I think they were telling us to get back up and fight."

Lorry offered me a wry smile. "I think the lady hawk was saying we'd strung it up all wrong."

"That would be the male hawk, saying that," I told her.

"Not if they're like us," she replied.

This was an unfinished—and unfinishable—argument. No one wore the pants in our family, because neither one of us want to wear them.

That evening, like all others for the next two weeks, we bathed in our freshwater pond, and while we were paddling idly among the lily pads and amethyst lilies that encircle it, I saw a female anhinga drying its wings on the white trunk of a fallen paperwood tree. I knew this because of the bird's characteristic tan head and neck. Both males and females, however, have black bodies with white plumes and silver edgings on the wings. The anhinga, or snakebird as they're often called, sat in that emblematic pose--wings extended, head erect. Her pointed bill was yellow and straight, unlike the cormorant that has a descending, hooked beak.

She was so still she appeared sculptural. I swam close enough to gaze into her red-orange eye. Her sun-gilt feathers were the gleaming black gown of an Egyptian queen. Like the heron of the night before, here was another Pine Island blessing. I admired the anhinga as I treaded water among the lilies. I don't know if she admired me, but I know she regarded me with tolerance. I could feel that she wasn't afraid of me. Like the hawks, with whom we were somehow bonded, this ancestral relative gave us a sense of both timely and timeless confidence in the renewal of life.

"It seems like a time of beginnings," I said to Lorry. "Everything is destroyed, and yet reborn. Everything is known, and unknown. Nothing is timid or afraid. All things are what they are. Only one day ago, the creatures were as strangers. Now they are relations."

That evening as we lay in bed trying to fall asleep in the oppressive night heat, the only sound was the far off barking of a dog, the nearby roar of a generator, and the crazy riff of a displaced mockingbird that kept waking up and singing for no reason other than joyousness.

We couldn't sleep. A poem by Richard Wilbur kept filtering through my mind. Its title was "Love Calls Us to the Things of This World." It was a poem about angels—things all around us that speak to us in the language of poetry and praise.

I told Lorry, "Angels are animals and birds, too."

"Sometimes they are little rose bushes," she added.

I thanked each of the flowered, feathered, furred and finned. For it was their love of life that had called us to the things of this world, and awakened us to our own inner strength.

Caya Costa Island
Southwest Florida (2006)

We lived on a barrier island off the mainland of Florida. It's a place where there are no condos and no-see-ums. We like it here. There's plenty to like and plenty not to like but once you get in the island groove you either don't want to come out of it or, for one reason or another, you can't. We have people named Mango Jack, Darryl With Teeth and Darryl With No Teeth. There are plain Darryls too but we don't count them. People have seen jaguarondis here and eighteen-foot saltwater crocodiles and Burmese pythons sometimes share the canals with monitor lizards as big as alligators. We also have a Win-Dixie Supermarket. I wrote "The Ancient Itch" for Gulfshore Life Magazine and it won an award. I got a lot of calls from toothless and toothful Darryls telling me to pipe down and not write so much. "You'll have people visiting us," they said. "Not as long as we have the ancient itch," I said.

A large green tropical iguana ran across Stringfellow Road yesterday, and I had to stop and look twice to see what it was.

Was it really an iguana?

Or rather, is this Southwest Florida?

The reality is that some of our unspoiled barrier islands (and even the well-combed ones like Gasparilla) are running wild with loopy lizards and other exotic runaway reptiles. We now have boas in the Everglades and monitor lizards that roam the north end of Cape Coral. The sometimes-six-foot monitors get into the mangrove fringes of Pine Island. I saw one the other day and did my usual double take: Was it, is it, where am I?

What author Paul Theroux said while kayaking here applies: "You can travel for days among the low and misleading islands on the outer reaches of Charlotte Harbor and never see a golfer, which I suppose is one definition of wilderness."

Our father-in-law, an avid golfer said, "You have it here, the wilderness. But what are you going to do with it?" I would answer like Carl Sandburg that there is a menagerie "…inside my ribs, under my bony head, under my red-valve heart." Having that wilderness inside myself, and this other one outside is a great comfort to me, and I don't always know, or care, the reason why.

Theroux handles his wilderness view with an eye to danger. He paddles innocently and eloquently, as if *imagining* Pine Island rather than *experiencing* it. Meandering in the network of waterways, barrier islands, Indian mounds and reptilian isles, Theroux paints a bas-relief of unmapped subtropical fantasy that is, nonetheless, our reality.

What he's talking about is the watery wilderness that precludes shopping malls, macadam main streets and designer domiciles. When roads of pitch black soften to white shell, when the heart of Florida can be felt within and without, our friend and fiend, the wilderness, is speaking directly to us. Our inner menagerie is under our rib cage, talking.

For some this may happen by merely glancing out a condo window at a panoramic view of the water. For others it may be seeing a footloose iguana, the kind you thought you would see in Ixtapa or Cozumel. Here the creature seems a bit out of context, and yet it is also appealing—to those people that like it. Florida has always had an eccentric wildness about it, a feeling that there are things growing here, even under your own skin, that don't belong. Things that beat to a different drummer, as it were. I call it the ancient itch.

When I first moved here, I had it bad. Well, to be perfectly frank, it sent me—this primordial itchiness—to a dermatologist, who, believe it or not, said I had a case of "bad sand." I could not define that. Neither could my dermatologist. He did say, however, that it was not something you got in Kansas. And he gave me some cream that had cortisone in it.

But my misplaced itch never went away. It's the thing under the skin that makes me love it here. I used to think low tide smelled bad—what did I know, I came from Santa Fe where the tide had gone away a million years before I got there. Now, I take a deep breath of that same mucky elixir and I get the old itch. "You gotta love it," my crab-happy neighbor says, "'cause there ain't nothin' like it." I've heard it put differently. I heard a guy getting off the plane say, "Ahm fixin' t'breathe some air that's thick enough to spread on toast."

"Where you been?" I asked him.

"Up North," he said.

I am called back to my ancient itch whenever I see creatures. Actually, I believe the presence of them, or the lack of them, defines our parameters of primal nature. We need them, not just to instill the ancient itch, but to keep it beyond the instant remedy of cortisone cream.

Alden Pines Golf Course on Pine Island is beautified with homes, but also remarkable animal populations that confound some of our more squeamish visitors. Some there are who don't enjoy seeing an Eastern Diamondback rattler coiled up in a bunker. And there are those who don't appreciate watching a common house cat lifted off its hind feet by a predatory eagle.

A few days ago, a friend invited us over to her house on a private estuary and while we were sipping a little rum on the lanai, a finch flew into the living room. Annoyed that the finch wouldn't leave, our friend began to clap loudly. "What's that for?" I asked. She answered, "I want the bird to fly out of here." I asked where their ladder was, got it, and climbed up to the highest window in the house where the poor finch was fluttering against the glass to escape.

I reached out and the bird was in my palm, its vibrant little body humming with sentient life, droning like a bumblebee with…the electrical impulse of the wilderness. When I set it free by opening my palm I remembered what a friend in Jamaica once told me: "A bird at sea has a wind vibration, a bird on land has a land vibration." This little golden finch still had its wind vibration and I felt it restoring my soul, seeping through my body and enchanting my heart. I felt it humming under my ribcage.

Thankfully, it's still here, the wilderness. Still with us. But can we keep from clapping and trying to make it go away? Can we refrain from trying to clap away the intrinsic, harmless nature that enters our lives? I don't really know. However, I hope we grow more patient; I hope the itch reminds us of who we really are. That we came, as Sandburg says, out of the wilderness, and it is to the wilderness we shall one day return.

I, for one, want the wild nature of the water in me until the day I die. "Life is good," quotes an Armenian poet friend of mine, "unless you weaken." I don't want to weaken, neither does he. That's why he also quotes his favorite Armenian proverb, "Making a living is like taking food from the tiger's mouth." Every once and a while, no matter what our age or respective financial position, we ought to gamble on a brief tussle in the woods or in the water—with something larger than ourselves.

I met a 97-year-old named Murph the other day who told me he couldn't swim in the Gulf anymore. Ruddy-faced and winsome, he laughed and added that his girlfriend, the same one who'd restricted his swimming, was twenty years his junior. He winked at me then. "She keeps me on my toes," he said with a quirky smile, "but she's forbidden me to swim with the sharks."

"Are you going to follow her orders?" I asked him. He chuckled, then said, "When I built my house back in the 1940s, A.J. Edwards— yes, the man himself—told me not to invest in Florida real estate because it wouldn't pay off. I just sold my last house for a million dollars, and they had to tear it down because it was old looking and small, and well, if A.J. couldn't drive me off the sand, how's my girlfriend going to drag me off the surf?"

I told him that I used to go for sharky dip off Casey Key in a weird little spot where I always got bumped by some hard, prehensile snouts. "It wasn't sharks, I told him, "but some finny fellows running from them".

"I know exactly where that is," he said. "You get hit by a bunch of mullet making their fast runs to the south. Once I saw something torpedo-shaped, chasing them, and it went right past me. I guess I'm too old and tough to be tasty."

A couple days after talking to Murph, I found myself on Caya Costa. The last thing on my mind that day was a "wilderness reckoning" but it happened, as it often does, when you're not expecting it to.

I was jogging across the width of the island in the late afternoon by myself, when I almost ran into a black feral sow and three little piglets with twitchy tails.

There was barely time for me to throw on my Adida brakes. Grinding to a halt, I stopped just in front of that monstrous, unmoving mama pig. A dark mist of flies swarmed around her head. She grunted. The sweat poured down my neck and trickled into my shorts. My heart was beating loudly.

Funny how things happen. You imagine you're at peace with nature, and then--*bam*—she's right there in your face. And her face doesn't look friendly. It looks truculent.

The first thing you do in such a situation is get calm. And then, if you're me, a whole waterfall of literature flows through your brain while you stand there sweating in the hot sun being examined by two mean little pig eyes in a vast hulk of hair and fat.

"There is a hog in me . . . a snout and belly . . . a machinery for eating and grunting . . . a machinery for sleeping satisfied in the sun—I got this too from the wilderness and the wilderness will not let it go."

Was it so unlike me, who almost ran into it? This grand thing of flank and snout and tusk and hoof?

I remembered the rest of Sandburg's poem: "I sing and kill and work: I am the pal of the world: I came from the wilderness."

And thus, I sat down on my own haunches, and took the weight off my mind and my body. The great sow cast a shadow over me and the long afternoon of golden green. I regarded her; she regarded me.

Centuries of nut eating, berry nibbling, lizard munching, bird and snake snatching had refined her genetics, and made her grandiose by any scale of the imagination. She was as big as a building.

For a brief moment, I visualized that building hurtling itself towards me and grinding me, mauling me into pulp mash.

All this life-flashing-before-me stuff lasted but seconds, yet seconds are eternities when your life is imagined to be on the line. That huge mama's eyes took me in. I saw her ears flicking, fanning flies. The piglets under her belly squealed; they wanted to move on. But before she did, that giant sow gave my head a brief sniff.

She smelled me. That monstrous-looking, blessed beast checked me out, and deciding that I was what she thought I was, she turned and trotted off into the jungled curtains of Caya Costa.

That night I got up from my favorite Pine Island easy chair, and picked up Theroux's *Fresh Air Fiend*. Finding the essay "Trespassing in Florida" I read about how Theroux "...nearly drowned...in one of the sudden storms that frequently explode over these islands." He describes being roughly a mile from dry land when a storm with 60 mph winds nearly outraced him to shore.

What I wanted to know was, how did he feel afterwards? After he made it safely to shore? Theroux doesn't really say. He writes "the mud flats, the mangroves and the mosquitoes, have in their way kept much of the area liberated, obscure, and somewhat empty..."

There is comfort in those words. For I'd never brag about running into a wild pig that could've rendered me into shreds of red, raw meat. I won't brag on my courage, or for that matter, my timidity, but I will always remember the peculiar, peaceful feeling that came afterward.

I truly felt Theroux's notion of being liberated, obscure, and somewhat empty like the land itself. The sense of knowing that the menagerie under my ribs hadn't *let* me down, but had in fact *sat* me down. The ancient itch was still in me, and it had seen me through another moment of truth. Once again I was one with the wild, the pal of the world, who didn't stick pigs, yet, for better or worse, was stuck to them by the wilderness.

Prague
Czech Republic (November 24, 2010)

The world has lost a great fighter for freedom. I refer to Jan Wiener, my friend of 41 years who recently passed away at the age of 90 in Prague. As a member of the internationally revered Czech Bomber Squadron of Britain's Royal Air Force, Jan was the last of a line, the last, in fact, of a breed of heroes we will not see again.

Much has been said about Jan Wiener's courage during the Second World War -- in books, films, and interviews. In Jan's own book *The Assassination of Heydrich*, he tells the story of how he and his father escaped Czechoslovakia when the Nazis had taken it over. They got as far as Ljubljana, Yugoslavia before the high-booted Storm Troopers marched in. "Tonight I will take the only way out," his father said. "I will commit suicide. My mind is made up. But I am worried about leaving you. It would be a great relief to me if you would join me -- but the decision is up to you."

As Jan explained, the two played a last game of chess. His father smoked a last cigarette. The endless boots marched beyond the door. "As a young man," Jan said, "I don't think it is natural to accept any situation as hopeless. After my father took his life with lethal white powder that he measured onto a piece of white paper, I realized my own situation. I was little better than a boy, alone in a strange place where the Gestapo were everywhere. I felt completely alone, completely helpless. For a moment, I too considered suicide."

But it was just a fleeting thought, he said. After which he determined to escape by rail. As it turned out, he stowed himself under a train, holding on with his bare hands to the iron stanchions beneath the toilet car where, now and then, there came a waterfall of excrement and urine that soaked him. Over bridges on high mountain passes, Jan held on, and on. It was his life he was holding on to, and his very breath depended on the strength of his hands.

Jan Wiener's narrow escape from the Nazis, and later, several prison camps in Italy is the stuff movies are made of. Therefore, it's not surprising that his life story has been depicted in the award-winning documentary film, *Fighter*.

*

When I think of Jan and the years we shared as teachers at the Windsor Mountain School of Lenox, Massachusetts where Jan came to work in the 1960s, I remember, most of all the phrases he used in so many daily occurrences. To be sure I was listening, he would say "Meat?" And I would answer "Bones".

This was the code that he used in a woodcutter's cabin in the mountains of Bohemia. He and his companion had stayed in a tiny cabin and after a long day of labor they would tell stories in the dark in their separate bunks. The word meat meant: "Are you awake?" Bones meant: "Yes, go on with your story!"

Meat and bones stories were exchanged by the two of us for many years. Once in *Night Flight*, a book I wrote about growing up in New Jersey, one of my characters, a man modeled after Jan says, "Jews are not a religion, a name, a nation. They are like a long sometimes lonely river that runs to the great sea, the ocean of humankind. Do you understand what I mean?"

Jan told me when he came to that part of the novel, he had watery eyes because he knew I was quoting something he'd said to me. "We are the same family, the same river," he said on his sunlit porch that day. I described Jan's rugged good looks in another paragraph: "He wore the same old country mustache like the handlebars on a racing bike, the silver hair with the sun coming in through the open roof touching it and making it glisten like alpine snow." For that, he smiled and said, "I am not Romany, like you." He also said, "I am an old fart, but I can still connect." By which he meant, with his fists. To the end, Jan was a brave and indomitable fighter. The size or force of the opposition was nothing to him.

He was, in fact, 25 years older than his wife-to-be, the beautiful Zuzana, who was but 13 when they met, and who told her mother that same day, "He's my type." The widowed mother, Wilma, thought the same. He was her type too. But it was Zuzana, some years later, who married him. Wilma said to Jan: "It is all right now, while you are still young, but what will you do when you are old and she is young?" To that, Jan said, "I will get a younger wife." He didn't. There was no need, for Zuzana stayed young and lovely, more so now than ever, after these many years.

Some people inspire in more ways than one. Jan was an inspiration to everyone who knew him. I knew many students at our school who wished not only to sound like Jan but despite their youth and his age, to look like him as well. I myself had a particular fondness for the way Jan spoke. His measured sentences, like the best prose, had the soft inflection of poetry.

Sometimes, over a glass of red wine, often *Bikaver* (blood of the bull in Hungarian), he'd recite the first paragraph of *A Farewell to Arms*. He spoke the one and two-syllable words, resonantly and methodically, so you could see the soldiers marching, the white dust of the roadbed rising and settling on the leaves of the trees and the coats of the soldiers. I think that by reciting that luminous paragraph, by doing it slowly and with quiet cadence, Jan taught me what it means to be a storyteller. And, saying that, I might add the word, Meat, in case he is listening somewhere and would do me the honor of letting the wind whisper, Bones.

Santa Fe
New Mexico (March 2010)

I have a friend, a distance runner, called Cloud Runner. He runs at high altitude -- 12 to 14 thousand feet -- and this has given him a mind that thrives on thin air and a body that glides like silk when he runs.

In a recent interview, Cloud Runner remarked, "I am now 67 years old. So I have been running most days for 55 years. It is a lifestyle, not an addiction. If I don't feel like it, I don't run . . . I don't keep track of how many days in a row, or how far I go in a year. Still, I have surely run 75,000 miles, and maybe 100,000."

Not bad mileage for a man with psoriatic arthritis. Now he has either beaten it or put up with it one cloud peak at a time. He mentioned that "A low dosage of methotrexate helped a lot, but it still hurt -- "yet I could run.

I decided that if I cut the dosage by a very small amount, too small for my body to notice, maybe I wouldn't go through withdrawal. This was necessary, I thought, because the drug, while helpful to me was also dangerous: it will slowly eat away the liver."

Today, he runs free of drugs, but not necessarily free of pain. But he says, "Diet has helped a great deal. I eat mostly fruits and vegetables, and organic meat in small amounts, using a vinegar marinade to help *pre-digest* the meat."

When asked about his daily regimen, he replied, "I have certainly not run more than fifty miles in a day." His answers are often like that. "I like to run," he says, "but I don't want to lose any sleep over it."

When I wanted to know if he hallucinated on any of his long-distance mountain runs, he replied, "The brain is hypoxic -- a deficiency of oxygen reaching body tissues at high altitudes. Different people are physically able to handle it differently. I wouldn't be surprised if some people hallucinate as a result. I don't. I also have no idea why that white mountain goat was jogging alongside me for several miles on Mt. Harvard."

I'd heard that Cloud Runner had been friends with Micah True, better known as *Caballo Blanco*, the fabled distance runner in the bestseller *Born to Run*. Micah recently died at the age of 59 while running in the Gila Wilderness in New Mexico.

True was a one-of-a-kind athlete. He modeled himself after the Tarahumara, arguably the greatest long-distance runners in the world. Like them, True liked to run in woven sandals; running one hundred miles was not strange to him. When he was found dead, staring up at the sky in a remote canyon his legend was intact. He died as he had lived.

Cloud Runner knew him, had run with him. Once on a camping trip in Los Alisos, Mexico, he heard True say, "One day I will go on a long run and not come back."

Cloud Runner added, "He was emphatic about it, prophetic, and I knew at the time it would be so. He may have known, or known instinctively, the way a runner knows his body, that he had heart disease."

I asked Cloud Runner if he looked up to Caballo Blanco more than any other back country runner and he said, "I most admire Tewanima, the legendary Hopi runner of the early 1900s. It was said that he would run from his village to Winslow, Arizona, a distance of 80 miles, just to watch the trains go by. It was said children would follow him out of town. Initially, his foot strikes were deep in the sand and a long stride apart. But as the village faded in the distance behind, the footprints became lighter and further apart until they disappeared altogether. One day, I will run in his footsteps."

12699 Cristi Way
Pine Island, Florida (1998)

Another memory I have is one I would sometimes like to forget. But the memory won't let me ... even now as I am typing, it pushes me to remember more.

The year Grandpa Roy stayed with us he thought the world was out to get him. It was. In his mind.

But his mind was fragmented by Alzheimer's.

One time he thought we were poisoning him and he snuck out of the house and told the neighbor on the other side of the pond that we were trying to kill him.

My friend and neighbor, Dick Newman, called us up and said, "You better come and get Grandpa, he's out of sorts, thinks you're poisoning him."

I went over and got him and that night he woke me up the way he always did by tapping me on the forehead. "There's a bear in the living room," he said.

I got out of bed and chased the bear away. The following night it was a werewolf. Grandpa said, "If you think I'm going to let a blood-thirsty werewolf tear apart this family, you have another thing coming."

The werewolf in question was our old dog, Mocha.

Grandpa got plenty of hugs and love from us and it wasn't that we ignored him or forgot to feed him or anything else. He was just an old career colonel who had a case of the heebie-jeebies as my neighbor Dick said. He also called it "Old Timer's disease" and CRS, which stands for, as everybody knows, "can't remember shit."

One bright, pretty Saturday morning when everything seemed calm and fine, Grandpa came into my workroom where I was working on a novel. He stared at me, his eyes boring into me as I typed. I stopped typing and he said, "Life is a dirty business and then you die." He let that sink in, but before it did, I said, "There is only life."

He glared at me. "Where did you get that?"

"From a Tibetan master at the meditation center in Santa Fe."

His eyebrows raised. "And you believed it?"

"I still do."

He shook his head. He had another plan, I could tell. "You have to get up early to deliver your newspapers," he said.

In the afternoon he saw a deadly snake outside.

I recognized right away that he was mesmerized by the Confederate Jasmine vine that was very close to the glass. The shape of the green frond was, I had to admit, a bit snaky.

"I'll just go outside and show you it's just a vine."

He tried to restrain me, holding on to my shirt. "If that thing bites you you're dead," he warned.

I shrugged, pulled loose of his grasp and went outside and took hold of the vine and shook it. "See, no snake!"

He stared in disbelief, his mouth open.

When I came back in, he said, "You took quite a chance there, young fellow."

The next day he was under the kitchen table shouting, "Get down! They're shelling again."

The following day, he stalked off with his grandfather's Colt revolver. My wife and I saw him go out the farm gate and head down the old shell road.

The gun didn't have a firing pin. It was an antiquated museum piece worth about 12 thousand dollars. We kept it in a frame, but he'd taken it out of the frame and was carrying it off with him. By his long strides I knew he meant business.

We got in our truck and drove all over looking for him. He wasn't anywhere. Nor did any of our neighbors know where he was. No one had seen him. Before we called the police, we got a call from someone up the road we didn't know. "Someone's here who maybe belongs to you people. I called Dick Newman and he said you had an Alzheimer's boy there, and so I called."

"Where is he now?"

"Sitting in my favorite chair with his favorite gun pointed at me."

"It's disabled," I told him. "I'll be right there."

"What were you thinking?" I asked Grandpa on the way home. "You know what that man said?"

Grandpa was glum. He shook his head like a boy who was being punished by his teacher.

"He said when he saw you outside by his mailbox with a drawn gun, he went and got his pistol and went out to meet you. People around here shoot first and ask questions later."

Grandpa sneered. "He's lucky I didn't shoot him. But he seemed like a nice fellow."

A few months after this incident Grandpa passed on in his sleep.

The last thing he said to me was, "Tell my wife I made it to the top of the mountain."

I couldn't tell her though because she had passed about seven years before and we'd scattered her ashes under a juniper tree. Those ashes made the moss under the tree flower and turn colors.

When we scattered Grandpa's ashes in the same place, I said aloud to the blue sky, "He wanted you to know he made it to the top of the mountain."

That night I was sound asleep when I felt a tap on the forehead. Opening my eyes, I saw Grandpa looking down at me. "I came back," he whispered, "to tell you that you were right."

"Right about what?"

"There is only life," he said.

And then he disappeared.

New Marlboro Road
Monterey, Massachusetts (1972)

I have always believed in miracles, large and small. Being alive is a miraculous event in itself. The greatest miracles come with signs. In Jamaica where we lived for many years, they say, Symptom and Sign. If this memory is not a symptom and sign of something miraculous, then I don't know what it is.

We bought our first house in the Berkshire hills. It had no heat or water. It was little more than a shell and it was 150 years old. But it sat on a hill encircled by large maple trees.

Strange to say now, we bought the house using our unused Mastercard. The house sold for 15 thousand dollars. With the card and our savings we had almost enough for the down-payment, but as it turned out, we were 500 dollars short.

This was the year of the gas crisis and the Nixonian eruption and we had just come through the wage and price freeze, and everyone we knew was broke. I told Karl, my oldest and best friend, that we had a great house we wanted to buy but were short of cash for the closing.

Karl said, "Look, Gerry, this sounds great, so go to Jenifer House and tell Cindy you need five hundred and she'll take it right out of the till and give it to you. Go get that house!"

We did that thing, with blessings for Karl and Jenifer House, his old New England Emporium of new-made antiques which, as Karl used to say, "Nobody needs and everybody buys."

We were in our ancient house a week later.

It was heaven on earth ... our first house.

But it had the two major drawbacks I mentioned: no water, no heat. And winter was approaching. The days were golden-leaved but the nights were chilly. More than chilly. Some nights were freezing cold.

So being a mountain man at heart, a lover of pain, basically, I dug a ditch from the house to the old hand-dug well behind the barn. I dug a 150-foot ditch three feet into the cold October earth.

Karl's son, Jed, a local builder of log cabins, came over. He surveyed the scene and then helped me with the hook-up. The only problem was this: Jed was pretty sure the old well hadn't been cleaned out in a century and it was full of leaf rot, moss, and woodland effluvia of all kinds.

"I'll lower you down 12 feet into the well," Jed said. "And you'll dig it clean with my Army shovel. You won't have much room down there so I hope you're not scared of tight enclosures."

"I can handle it."

Jed got the shovel and some strong rope and he lowered me down into the eyehole of the well. I wrote a poem about it some years later.

Cleaning Out the Old Man's Well

There is always the fear
Of who I am down there

Me stuck in that hole –
The sink a man put
In a green field
To feed his blue eyes

I stare crazily up
At my helper
Who, on the very rim of sky
Tosses me a second rope
Into the hole

My feet are stuck
In muck
I can't move

Froze in ooze
A helluvaway
To lose

Dig, Jed says,
For life
And I'll pull

For all I'm worth
He did
And I'm here

To tell that water
Line lasted
One flush.

I "borrowed" water from October to December from our next-door neighbor Harold Hart, who was a direct relation of William Shakespeare's wife, Anne Hathaway. What a generous man Harold was. We literally hooked a hose up to the side of our house and had water, he said, as long as we wanted to use it. I say prayers to Harold at least once a day.

However, just as the well went dry so did our finances. I mean completely dry. I took an early winter's house painting job with my friend Jon Graboff and I made runs to Manhattan to do editing for various publishers. One of them was Freeway Press.

Freeway was run by Maurice Girdodius. He was the son of Jack Kahane who founded the Olympia Press in Paris and published Anais Nin, Henry Miller and many other authors from the 1930s.

Gerard Malanga, my friend and best friend of Andy Warhol, also one of the best poets in America, got me the job. But he warned me, "Cash Maurice's checks as soon as he writes them. Right on the spot. In fact get him to cash them. He keeps a lot of cash in the top drawer of his desk."

"Why don't I ask for my pay in cash and save the trouble."

Gerard gave me his million-dollar Velvet Underground smile (he did the whip dance in the group), and said nothing.

I wrote two pornographic novels for Maurice for which he always paid me 750 dollars per book. The first novel was called The Godfather and it was based on a book written in the 19th century. There was sex in it but I ramped it up and made it more exciting. I had a nun and a priest making love in a vineyard and getting all tangled up in vines. Maurice complained that even his father wouldn't have published it.

Freeway Press, despite having a mass market best seller written by Mohammad Ali and another one by Harpo Marx, failed and went underground. Then it went out of business.

My last check from Maurice was pushed through Berkshire Bank eleven times. It was finally cashed the last time we pushed it through and the teller, looking at all the red stamps on it, said, "You better frame this one." I did that, too. Money of the misbegotten but it got us through most of the winter months. That and Harold's gift of water. Which reminds me of Oberon Zell's "Brother, will you drink water with me?" but that's another story, better told by my friend Gregory Pearl Pleshaw.

So when we were out of money again, I took to praying.

I prayed often, too.

One night I went up on the hill opposite our house and prayed so hard it hurt my head. But after about a half hour of prayer, I opened my eyes and saw a magnificent green streak pass right over our house and light up the woods far away, somewhere off near Tyringham.

The next morning the phone rang bright and early. I answered it. A woman on the other end explained that I had been selected as a possible poet in residence at Connecticut State College in New Britain.

I was stunned. My hand was shaking. I could barely hold the phone.

"What do I do, then?" I asked.

"We'll call you for an interview."

"When will that be?"

"Later this afternoon."

"May I ask how many other poets have been selected for this honor."

"We have thirty-five poets being interviewed."

I took a deep breath.

And then I remembered the green streak passing over the house.

"May I ask what the sinecure is?"

She laughed. "It's 500 dollars a week."

In 1972 that was a lot of money.

Even today it is a lot of money.

I drove our Volkswagen to New Britain that afternoon and saw a whole lot of familiar faces. Which is to say, out of work poets that I knew from former times.

When the line thinned and I found myself confronting the Dean, she smiled, and said, "Don't be so nervous, you have the job."

"What about the others?"

"That," she said, "is a formality required by the grant. You have the job."

Traveling

The Windsor Mountain School
Lenox, Massachusetts (1970);
St. Thomas, Virgin Islands (1970, 2010);
Cinnamon Bay, St. John's Virgin Islands (1970)

One of my first revelations as a teacher during my first year teaching was that my students could disappear off the face of the earth.

That is a hard truth for a new teacher to accept.

Your students could die before you?

Even more amazing to me was that the brilliant, the exceptional, the sometimes genius students could vanish without a trace. I still wonder about Bill Place, who one day walked out of the classroom where I was teaching Gary Snyder's poetry. I stopped teaching, went to the door where Bill had exited and said, "Where are you going?" and he answered "That's what I'm trying to find out." I never saw him again. I wonder if he is alive. Somehow I don't think so. My first year teaching I lost a dozen students in a similar fashion and when the school necrology list appeared after 25 years, there were over a hundred names on it. What follows is a true story.

I am standing on the streets of St Thomas looking for Blackbeard. He's out there somewhere with bluebirds in his beard and fiery dreadlocks and a mouth of missing teeth.

Diane was in the next room, tangled in sheets, naked with my wife. They weren't having sex or anything, just two girls sleeping. The whole trip was sad and insane. Our friend, Win had just died in St John, and we were going over there from St Thomas for his funeral. Just various people coming and going and saying goodbye to Win who had been in a car wreck. He and Paul and Marsha had gone off the same damn cliff. They were high of course, stoned on acid, ganja and rum, unconditionally stoned, and over they went all three. The rental car crashed on a rock and Paul and Marsha hung on as sharks slashed at their feet. It wasn't much of a rock and the car was on most of it and Win was dead.

All three of them were poets just as Diane was a poet and so am I; and Lorry's the poem that writes itself in the way she is. I think poets can get into more trouble than any other kind of people -- witness Poe, Rimbaud, and Verlaine, not to mention Plath and -- oh, who cares, my point is well taken, I think, if not my advice on why we shouldn't all be poets. They killed themselves, they kill themselves, one way or another, they do themselves in. Diane did, later on. Not that much later on, but sometime after our trip.

St Thomas I'm walking your crooked streets and the songs are bursting out of my belly and I can't hold them in anymore. I am looking for Webster's winged chariot, I am looking for anybody who's still alive. I am looking. I am good, looking, and so is everyone else on this island. We get a serendipitous ride from a madman named Webster. He drives like a whore on fire who's trying to put the fire out with wind. Webster's Bonneville's got a ragin' eight-cylinder engine and glittery chrome hand controls -- he works the lot with his hands -- jerking the brakes, gas pedal, and of course the floor shifter that's up real high so he can downshift fast and scream those tires and blow blue smoke out back and his chariot hurtles through the Caribbean void of Blackbeard's beard and we're nighttime marauders on the lunatic fringes of foam, ganja-fueled partners of the reefy night. And so down to the docks where we board the ferry as the sun reddens the horizon and casts roses on the sea. Bye, bye Webster, you scared the shit out of all three of us but you brought Win right back into our hearts and he's been there ever since.

The rock where Win died overlooks Cinnamon Bay. The morning after the crash, Paul told Marsha whose leg was crushed and bleeding, that he'd swim to shore and get help. The tide was high and creeping up the rock. Paul swam. The sharks stayed close to the rock and Marsha's blood spoor. Paul got lost in the jungle of St John. Don't forget, he was high on acid and ganja, but mostly acid. He walked through the doors of perception holding hands with Jim Morrison, and disappeared into the wilderness and didn't come out for three days.

Marsha almost died on that rock. I say almost because she lived. When they found Paul among the feral cats and tree rats of the interior, the police took him to jail and locked him up. He kept screaming in his delirium about someone named Marsha, and they finally found her, the real girl, and got her to a hospital and saved her life. Now Diane and Lorry and I were casting roses into the waves and waiting to see if the tide carried them out to the dock. It does. Sweet Jesus. Goodbye Win.

Win doesn't say goodbye so easily. That's for those who believe in closure, whatever that is -- whatever we want it to be, I guess. Things don't close in nature; they stay open like the doors of perception, like Morrison's poems, like the Caribbean sky full of malice and tears. Win comes into the tent where Diane and Lorry and I are sleeping naked in the heat and I am watching their nipples burning darkly in the dawn when in walks Win. He's a dog. Not a phantom. Not a man or a boy. A real big scruffy island dog, but he talks in the smooth, gentle, breathy tones of Win, my student, whom I loved. "Win, you're gone," I say. He talks like Joe Hill -- "I never left," says he. The big dog talks, turns around, leaves. Then it pisses all around the tent. I can hear it squirting rum-piss on the taut canvas, and I'm thinking --that'll keep the airborne night rats at bay.

Back in St Thomas, I called home and my mother said that my father was dying. I talked to him. The connection is weak, his soft voice seems to be spiraling through the convolutions of a queen conch shell. "Keep your hat on and your feet dry," he told me.

I was full of death then, brimming with it, soaked to the bone with death, as if in fact there were no such thing as life, as if the concept of life were Death's joke. To prove that I existed at all, I searched the city for a man named Tram Combs, a poet who owned a bookstore. He had my book of poems in his store and I wanted to see it in the window, hoping that it would be there, because he apparently liked it, especially the Nevis Mountain poems.

But as hard as I looked (Webster was driving, that has to be the reason) I couldn't find Tram's store, and I never met him or my book in the window smiling cheerily in the window as I imagined it would be, but when I got home Tram had ordered more copies. Who was buying them? Webster?

This all happens forty years ago and Paul's rich and living in West Palm and somewhere in his late fifties and Diane's dead of an overdose and Lorry and I have been together now all forty of these forty-odd years, and add four more. Marsha's alive, somewhere, with a limp. Win's ghost's gone -- dog no more. He came back one more time to tell me that, and then no more Win.

But forty years later, I am back on St Thomas and I am singing in the street -- fifteen men on a deadman's chest yo ho ho and a bottle of rum drink and the devil had done the rest yo ho ho and a bottle of rum. And I am still looking for Blackbeard with bluebirds in his beard, and I am still searching for Webster's winged chariot of fire, and out of the misty morning, Lorry and I see a cab driver who might, or might not, be Webster.

"Are you Webster?" I ask.

He smiles. "You mean that old guy with the Pontiac. Him long gone, mon. Long time me nuh see him."

"I knew him," I say.

"We all know Webster," he replies. Then, "You really know him?"

"Ever ride at dawn in a fast Bonneville heading to the docks and your driver's got no legs and he's really speeding and you're wondering if the car's got no brakes?"

The gray-haired driver busts out with a laugh. Eyes damp with tears, he says, "You know him. You know him, mon. Long time him gone."

From Germany to Jamaica;
From the Midwest to Miami (1995-2015)

I traveled all over this country, the Caribbean and Europe telling stories from many cultures. I also spoke on NPR and Pacifica Broadcasting and History Channel. My stories were recorded on seven audio books, and you could say I got around a little bit on and off the airwaves.

Doing storytelling for kids is a balancing act. You never know exactly how you're going to go over, or precisely what you're going to do or say. It's a lot like riding waves in a tropical storm. Into the trough and up, up into the air!

In Germany a boy said, "You're a pretty good writer and all that, but did you ever get a medal?"

I scratched my head and said no.

At the end of the young writer's conference there was a farewell address given to the various writers in attendance and as it turned out I was called to the podium. The same blond boy who asked the question presented me with a brass medal that now hangs on a red, white and blue ribbon right next to my computer.

I recall doing a storytelling in Miami some weeks later and I had to compete with Clifford, the Big Red Dog. Then a boy asked me if I could do Donald Duck. I tried, I swear I did. It sounded OK to me but the kid burst out laughing and did a Don Duck that sounded like a soundtrack from Disney.

You never know ... at a gifted school in North Miami, I was asked to read from my book *How Chipmunk Got Tiny Feet* and after every story, a first grade boy in a blue school uniform stood up and said, "I read that story. I didn't care for it."

Every single time, there he was proclaiming my inadequacy as a writer. Well, OK. The final time he stood up and said, "I didn't care for it" I said: "Well it didn't care for you either." The boy sat down. His teacher came over to me as I was packing to leave and said, "You did well to put him in his place. He's just repeating what his father says about everything he sees or hears. You just told him that things work both ways, thank you!"

When I got home there was a letter from a guy in jail in Georgia. "I read your book," he said. "I had nothing else to do."

But then writers get all kinds of letters. Some good, some bad, some downright threatening. A man blamed me for killing his mother. She was found with my book in her lap, dead. He took the time and trouble to tell me in twelve pages that my novel had killed her. I wrote him back and said she'd obviously died of boredom.

And there was the letter from the friendly, good-hearted lady who said she'd found a cache of letters at the town dump where her father worked. They were love letters from my mother to my father. She said they were the most beautifully written letters she'd ever read and would I like to have them back.

How do these things happen?

So I had my mother's love letters.

But not my father's.

And then my cousin found my father's love letters to my mother in her horse barn.

We put both sets of letters, side by side in a book which will be published in the next year.

A gentleman by the name of Brent Glass said he's read the book I wrote about Hugh Glass and John Colter and that it was so accurate he got a clear sense of what his relative was really like. A member of the Colter family said the same except she felt we should have described John Colter's ears a little better. I am not making this up.

We, my wife and I, as co-authors, received a letter from a member of the family whose relation was on the Titanic the night it went down. The letter-writer said, "Our family would like to ask you to take out the dog in the Titanic story. Our relation had no dog."

Another letter from an admirer said, "I saw your wolf quote on a bronze plaque next to a statement made by Mother Theresa and Henry David Thoreau. Nice work."

A lawyer who was writing in behalf of Beverly Last Horse wrote to me saying that the photograph of Samuel Last Horse on the cover of my book of legends, *Tunkashila*, was appreciated. Especially since the family had not seen Samuel for a century.

As it turned out, Samuel's image was reprinted by a stationery company around 1903 when Samuel was traveling with a Wild West Show. The person who had bought the stationery had written a letter in Old German. I had tried but failed to find a translator for it.

However, I liked the handsome face of Samuel Last Horse and also the unusual handwriting that accompanied it. At a reading I gave in a church in the South, a man came up to me and said the script on the book cover was talking about the drought and I said, "That's curious, because Samuel Last Horse was a Thundermaker who could have ended that drought."

Things happen to writers that might not happen to others. It's something to do with the effort one makes to reach out and touch distant souls in distant places.

Once I read a story from my YA novel *Doctor Moledinky's Castle* to a large group of high schoolers in a cafetorium in northern Georgia. A week or so later someone mailed me an Associated Press clipping from a newspaper about a "chicken cult" in the town where I had given my reading. *Moledinky's Castle* is, among other things, about a boy who falls in love with a pretty girl named Pam Snow who collects chicken heads on a chicken farm in New Jersey. It's a gruesome lovely romantic story about a real girl I knew in high school. Sales of the book did not increase. I still have a few copies left.

The other day a man wrote me this: "Please send specific instructions to the place where Uton climbed The Jacob Ladder in Jamaica. I am staying near the Ladder, but I cannot find it."

"I love your story about the magic chair and the boy and girl who go flying together on it. Is that true? My sister and I need to know." – What writer wouldn't like to have that said about his book? But this …" I have waited ten years for the sequel to your novel Stargazer. What are you going to do about it?"

I wrote her back and said. "I am at work on it right now."

Strangely, it took me about ten years to finish the series (I still have two to go) but this devoted reader phoned me once each year to say,

"Hurry up, I'm waiting."

Better than that, the woman in Long Island who sent me a picture of her cat sleeping on our collection of cat stories. She said it was the last picture taken of her cat while it was alive.

Then she said, "Would you teach at my school if I built it?"

I would, I told her.

I will.

Will you build it?

Hurry up, I'm waiting.

From Mavis Bank, Jamaica to Brooklyn, New York; From New Mexico to Cesky Krumlov, Czech Republic; From Ramstein Air Force Base, Germany to Macon, Georgia (1993-2000)

My old Doc Marten hiking shoes have been places. I went to the top of the Blue Mountains with them. I was up there among the orchids and hailstones, and then I went up higher to where the trees were smaller and twisted by the wind, and then it was all wind and grass. I've always been afraid of heights, so I felt more comfortable sitting down in the tall grass and listening to the wind moan. You could see the blinky lights of Kingston twiddling on and off in the cloud cover eight thousand feet down below. It started to snow and these shoes got me to a plateau where the snow wasn't falling. There were acres of cheese berries all along the trail, and we browsed like goats.

A Rastaman who worked for the Mavis Bank Coffee Co. came by and said his name was Tiger. "What you see up top?" he asked. He was testing to see if we'd gone all the way up. I was full of cheeseberries and feeling full and easy, and I said, "Well, there's a little cabin up there and Steve Marley wrote his name on the roof. That's what I saw." Tiger's eyes crinkled at the corners and he laughed. "You were up dere."

I am still wearing these shoes as I write and they're more than fifteen years old and I'm thinking of sending this as soon as I finish writing it to Doc Martin and tell him how much I appreciate wearing this one singular pair of his shoes for fifteen years.

I was wearing these shoes the day the stock market crashed -- the first time -- back at the turn of the present century. Who knows how many times I've worn these shoes since the market crashed all these other times after the first crash. I think all it ever does is crash and recover, crash and recover. I lost a hundred grand and kept these shoes. So I could land on my feet.

I was wearing these shoes for what they were calling "the storm of the century" before the real storm of the century named Katrina -- this was in 1993 when that nor'easter punched the lights out of Manhattan and I was staying in Brooklyn wearing these shoes and the only safe place out of the monster wind was a movie house where we hunkered down, me and two bums, and stayed warm and toasty watching a movie all to ourselves. I hoped they had shoes as good as mine and as weatherproof because my feet weren't wet at all.

I walked out on to the street and the snow was up to my knees and I was wearing my agent's duster and underneath that, a down vest and I was warm and dry in these shoes. Me and my agent, we had a thing going, not exactly a romance because I was happily married but we were best-best friends and we talked on the phone ten times a day and I loved hearing her voice and one day she said, "I have a feeling you're going to make me a lot of money."

I was wearing these shoes when she said that. Well, basically, I didn't. Make a lot of money. But I did wear these shoes a lot that year and I traveled everywhere. I was wearing these shoes in Germany when some people in Hohenecken heard my last name, and then the whole bar toasted me for having the name Hausman. That happened in France, too, on account of there being a Hausmann Boulevard in Paris. I burned a lot of shoe rubber that year.

I realize, in praising these shoes, I have done a disservice to my agent's duster. It was a large coat and she was a large woman. Inside her coat I felt small, like a mouse in a circus tent and sometimes she would be talking on the phone to people like Ray Bradbury and Robert Bloch and I'd be sitting there wiggling my mousey toes in these shoes and wondering where she was going to send me next. She had plans and I was her soldier -- in these shoes. Yes, my agent was a large handsome woman who summoned large advances. But that's an exaggeration unless you consider how poor I was starting out and finishing up. I didn't mind the sort of arty poverty; I wasn't Ray Bradbury or anything. But I did love my agent. In the way that authors do. She made great vegetable soup, too.

I wore these shoes for the big literary life that wasn't that big, but there was a black limousine from time to time that Simon & Schuster paid for from time to time, and I liked the Ukrainian driver because he reminded me of my camp counselor Romand Veronka who used to go down the rapids at breakneck speed and he'd pee off the stern of the canoe while were shooting the white water. The black limousine driver did that in the snow in Brooklyn.

I was wearing these shoes during and after Hurricane Charley that hit Pine Island on August 13, 2004. Charley was a very bad boy. He tore up trees and replanted them miles away. He taught fish to swim in the sky, and he bashed our house pretty good but not as bad as our neighbor's who lost roofs, walls, and, well, houses. I wore these shoes at night and fell asleep in chairs I was so tired of sawing pine trees. But I could shine these shoes and have them look brand new and do a storytelling and earn some money, and these shoes never needed any repair and no one ever said -- "Why do you always wear those old beat-up shoes?"

I wore these shoes when my three grandchildren were born in Miami and I wore them with Cedella Marley when I performed with her onstage at The Kennedy Center.

I wore these shoes when I was hired to tell stories in the city of Birmingham, Alabama and I walked in them to the church where the innocents were murdered and, too, I wore these shoes in New Orleans where these shoes sang the blues and I was wearing these shoes when I heard the Gypsy fiddles of Cesky Krumlov caves in the Czech Republic, and all up and down the streets of Prague drinking ice chilled slivovitz and giant glasses of Pilsner.

I have to say, though, that these shoes have no memory of any of these things. They don't know night from day as they're giving lifetime service and always looking good and never appearing to be tired or broken down or luckless or any other thing you might name that would be a disparagement to shoes, in general. These shoes cover my toes in good and bad weather for richer or poorer, wellness or want, debt or darkness, love or light, and I love these shoes because my feet fill them with the strangeness that is me and I am still wearing these shoes.

St Thomas, Kingston, Basseterre, Charlotte Amalie, Nassau to Christmas in Old San Juan, Puerto Rico (2010)

What is the muse? Is she, as some say, an angel? Is she a figment of the imagination? Is she a corporeal human being who visits once in a lifetime? Is she your wife, daughter, sister, best friend? I met her once in Old San Juan. It was a short but life-changing meeting of fire and frenzy. The city was lit up with purple and blue lights. There were folk ensembles and bands on every street. Drummers on every corner, folk trios with twelve string guitars, congas, bongos, steel drums, and passing over the cobbles on light, dancing feet--the prettiest women. Age did not stop any of them from hip-swaying, laughing, singing, dancing, drinking, and having a good time. We saw the tallest woman in the world and the shortest on the same street and they were both flirting with the stars and that old, mischievous San Juan moon peeking over the wrought-iron, ancient balustrades of the heavy-eyed, sleepless city. We watched the tiny woman throw her head back and laugh at the moon--she was no bigger than a cotton mouse. And then the tall, African queen danced close to the mouse, as if they were sisters and the queen's gown was green sequins and her skin changed like an anole's from blue-gray in shadow to honey gold in the moon and her hips and shoulders flicked to the rhythms, and far beyond the coquina-mortared walls of the city, the banana leaves lapped the cool sea air and drank darkness. Then a fire dancer, a blue-haired mime who couldn't have been more than sixteen, played with fiery batons throwing them over her head, around her back and through her legs. She had wild blue hair and we feared she'd set it afire but she didn't. She danced and burned and disappeared. And after she was gone the fast replay of her fire-hustling moves kept coming back. Where was that angel of the blue-haired Puerto Rican night? We looked for her but she was nowhere and yet she was everywhere--in everything we touched, heard, smelled and dreamed, not just that night but after days at sea still there on the edge of all that is.

—

Oceanside, Oregon and
Prague, Czech Republic (1999-2006)

Children's book writer David Greenberg once said jokingly to me, "I am feeling a little bit Jew-ish, how about you?"

I was thinking about David's sense of humor when, just this morning, I found a review written by an internet troll who called me, "A lying Jew bastard."

Curious about what compelled such a ridiculous appellation, aside from ignorance and prejudice, I wondered if the very name Hausman triggered this response.

Some hours later, I discovered a family heritage that I had forgotten about. Namely, (so to say) the fact that Hausman is what might be called a Jewish name, as well as a German one.

However my family, on my father's side, came from Zemplén, Hungary. On my mother's side, they came from Plymouth, Massachusetts, and before that, jolly old England. Yes, Mayflower folks, and in fact, the first family to be legally married in Plymouth. In the words of an editor of mine: "On the Jewish roster, that makes you nothing. It's got to come from the mother's side."

Still, I feel "a little bit Jew-ish." And I do recall being at an editorial meeting in Manhattan where the director of affairs, the head of a major mass market publishing company said, "Well, here we are. We're all Jews and we're all smoking." He meant cigarettes, as was the editorial fashion in the 1970s.

Back to the name Hausman ... It was my friend Jan Wiener, whose family was wiped out by the holocaust, who took me to the "Name Buying Street" in Prague.

"This is a street like the one in Hungary where your family probably bought the name Hausman," he said. Jan added, "Names that sounded good were actually purchased as early as the Hapsburg dynasty. There were name-buying streets in Hungary as well as

Prague, and other cities in Europe. A good name was worth a lot. You didn't want to lug around a name like Schnitzelgruber or Katzenellenbogen. This became especially true in the New World at the turn of the last century."

Jan was an historian as well as a freedom fighter, author, and Jew.

"Your heritage is secure," he told me. "Your line of lineage comes down from both parents. We don't have to follow that rigid orthodox formality -- 'It's got to come from the mother's side.'"

I was amused by a Pueblo Indian elder from New Mexico who asked me what my background was and I told him directly, and he laughed. "You're just a fruitcake like all the rest of us." Some time after he said this, my lifelong Navajo friend, Ray Brown, said "I would like to hear about your native heritage."

I told him my mother's family had some "American Indian blood", and he chuckled. "Who cares about that? I want to hear about the first natives, the first wanderers, the oldest tribe of all, the Jews of Genesis. Got any of those in your family?"

It was around the same time that my D.A.R. great aunt said, "Someone told me your mother married a Jewish person. I told them that was not true."

So, down we come to the fact we are all a bunch of fruitcakes, first wanderers, and happy-go-lucky, once upon a time, name buyers. That makes us all, if we like, "a little bit Jewish."

Fort Lauderdale, Pascagoula, Mason, Texas (2016)

After 22 years of living on a barrier island off the West Coast of Florida, my wife and I decided to move back to the place we came from -- Santa Fe, New Mexico. There are four of us in a 1993 Ford F-150 pickup truck. I am driving. To my right on the seat is Mouse, our 15 year old diabetic dachshund who is now almost totally blind. Next to Mouse is Lorry, and in the back of the cab is George, our 37-year-old Blue-fronted Amazon parrot. We have had George since he was a baby, a wild bird stolen from a nest somewhere in Mexico and given to us by a Lutheran minister in Santa Fe.

We are the most unlikely animal family on the road right now and cars passing us sometimes stare. First night out, heading towards Fort Lauderdale, we somehow find ourselves lost in the dystopian landscape of a truck stop. A hundred engines are growling. We park and listen to the guttural roar of the truck stop night.

It's midnight at Joadie's Cafe and Strip Club. The night is wet from a recent rain and the puddles are lakes. It is always summer in these regions of congested America in Florida. We watch, all four of us, as silk-vested men with pencil mustaches overstep the puddles and then slink through the neon night to Joadie's.

How much I would give to be a fly on the wall in that hole in the wall.

Mouse is stoic. She waits for her next insulin injection. George chortles. He can see what's going on in Joadie's. He doesn't like it, except to cackle at it in his sinister way.

Let me explain something about George. To him, clothes are feathers. He thinks we humans look okay in our variable feather clothing. But George loathes people who divest themselves of their feathers. He can see that something of this nature is going on at Joadie's. Feather disrobing is such a no-no with George that he screams. His raucous screech splits the night. Some sleepy-eyed truckers roll down their windows and glower, fat-faced and -- forgive pun -- truculent.

Ah, George ... I well remember the time he attacked someone in our house who ran from bathroom to bedroom naked as a jaybird. (George hates jaybirds, but more so, naked human bodies.) He has attacked bald men just for being naked-headed. "Get yourself some head-feathers," he rasps.

And that reminds me -- George *really* talks. Once he watched a TV murder mystery with me where the villainous husband of a victimized woman was shot dead. George watched in surprise as the mean bastard bit the dust, and then George said, "What happened to the poor man?" When he wants to George can speak the king's English.

His disgust at Joadie's skin parlor causes him to croak, "Cover up!" Then he adds, "Nite-nite." He says this in an innocent little kid's voice.

We put an old Army blanket over his cage.

It is in Pascagoula though, where George, for some reason, feels at home. Pascagoula, a tribal bend in the wide lonesome river where the people known as "the breadeaters" once made their village in the long ago. Legend has it they honored a mermaid deity. Rather than give in to a Spanish priest who tried to convert the tribe, they joined the fish woman in Biloxi Bay and forever disappeared. This story is told to us by a Mississippi man named Zip.

Another night in the soft, whimpering wilderness that Henry Miller once called "the air conditioned nightmare" we eat at a Waffle House and then repair for the night at a Super 8 where there is as much mischief as Joadie's midnight cafe and truck stop strip club. Mouse begs pizza at midnight in Pascagoula. We give tiny pieces and she shares them with George who walks, well, pigeon-toed to the feast. Then the old blind dachshund beds down on her sheepskin that we carry from place to place -- it being her only safety in this chaotic world of lostness -- and George settles down next to Mouse and I hear him say, "This is for you when you wake up, I know you can't talk now."

La Grange
Texas (2016)

After seven straight hours of hell driving through griddle hot Houston, we arrive in the dark at La Grange, Texas. We are George the parrot, Mouse the dachshund, and Lorry and me. I am road blind, sun blind, weary unto death.

So we stop at the first motel we see. It's quite a ways off the main drag. The signs around the place -- some neon, some not -- say, *Well Come, Frens!* Tired though I am, I notice that the motel spells it *Bait* on some signs and *Baits* on others.

Time to crash.

We have resigned ourselves to do nothing but sleep. The room is a small broken-down adobe on a side alley where scrawny dogs slink into the shadows away from our headlight glare.

Okay, so it smells like my uncle Willie's unwashed underwear -- this rundown room that is to be our overnight home away from home.

So we pay fifty bucks for an eight by eight migrant shack with no windows -- they are all boarded up and painted blue to scare off the werewolves and witches.

Are we the bait of the Baits Motel?

Lorry opens the fridge and it is blue with mold. Well, at least the color is coordinated with the boarded-up windows.

And on top of a 1950s b/w TV there is an insouciant cockroach picking his teeth. The TV doesn't work. The AC unit wheezes and coughs with such cacophony, we turn it off and endure the paint-blistering Texas heat.

Lorry states facts: "I will not undress in this place, nor will I get under the covers even if attacked by tarantulas!"

"Of which there must be many," I add.

George cackles from his perch: "What it is."

"Yes," I reply, "but what is it?"

"What it is," he answers.

In the bathroom there are two tiny towels stolen from Motel 6. Lorry sniffs them. "Mold and more mold," she says. We decide, after all those hours of sweaty driving, to take a shower, for better or worse. The shower must have been a storage unit for coal, either that or another mold garden. The cockroach joins us, we jump out leaving the cockroach to dance by himself. We dry ourselves with our crummy, sweaty T shirts.

Surprisingly the bathroom, so-called, has a tiny window and it is open a crack. I crack it wider and see some old men crouched around a steel barrel emitting fountains of evil-smelling coal smoke. I try to shut the window but it won't shut. There is an explosion of laughter from the old men. They're telling jokes. George thinks this is really funny and he starts laughing, very gratingly, with them. They are silent for a moment, then they laugh even louder than George, and George laughs louder than them, and Lorry says, "Let's get out of here."

But we don't. We decide instead to try to beat the odds, and sleep. After all, Mouse, the dachshund is happy on her sheepskin bed. George is still chuckling with the old men of the smoking barrel, and as they say, we're all in this together.

I suppose, by lying down on top of the moldy smelling mattress in our clean clothes, we have passed the dharma test. Life is suffering. We suffer, they suffer, we all suffer.

All except Mouse who is snoring, treading the light fantastic, having dreamy dreams of happy fleece.

All except George who whispers, "What it is."

And, finally, in his bleariest Baits motel voice, "Nighty night."

On the Llano River
Mason, Texas (2016)

After La Grange, we find ourselves dispirited, exhausted.

We need a rest, a real rest, and so we head to our artist friend Bill Worrell's compound on the Llano River.

This is mesquite country, remote and lovely and Bill is a great host, giving us a guest cottage under the fruit trees. If we squint we can see the big green river through the trees.

After a good night's sleep, George is up early, grawking and begging for breakfast. We carve up some sweet rolls for him and sip our coffee. Bill's guest cottage has a view of the miles of mesquite through the glass door facing west. First thing, George begins to talk: "What're you doing there anyway?"

We think he's talking to us until we find out that he conversing with a roadrunner in the backyard. A quick footed, sharp-witted ground bird with an eye to a meal called Snake. We watch the wiry and wily bird crank a snake breakfast out of a hole while George invokes the Fifth, yelling madly, "Help, Hannah, Black Dog, Police!"

Hannah's our youngest daughter and for some reason she always gets called in an emergency. Black Dog went to his reward twenty-five years ago – no telling why he always hollers for his help. Police he got from TV, also because it's easy to say and makes a good yell.

The morning is full of redbird whistles, songs and cheers in addition to George's field hollers. But watching the roadrunner pull apart a snake reminds of what poet Philip Whalen said about the predatory groundbird: "Try to take it away from him," he said in one of his best poems.

George tries to take it away from him, auditorally.

His loudmouth admonishments would scare anyone and might even bring Black Dog back from the grave. But Roadrunner stands his ground. Doesn't move an inch except to tear apart the snake.

After this confrontation, the large bird makes a run for it. Is something bigger coming? In fact, it is: five small East Indian deer with snow-spotted markings. Beautiful creatures. They stay in the pear blossom shadows for a minute or two and then move on.

Bill's paradise is quite a contrast after Baitsville.

Bill, the Texas storyteller, fine art painter, author of bestselling books, country songs and inventor of Go-Cooker, an Edisonian bit of brilliance. It's a cookpot that attaches to your automobile exhaust pipe and stews up a delicious dinner while you drive a nice little distance.

We love Bill and his Llano preserve, and so does Mouse.

George is preparing mean oratory for the next meeting with Roadrunner, but we have to cut short the visit and move on because we are due in Tesuque, New Mexico in another 24 hours. Besides Bill has more company coming and the elbow room is narrowing.

Back on the road, Mouse sits on Lorry's lap and pants in the Texas heat. Our AC is not working. We drive, windows down, back to our old homeland in New Mexico. It's empty prairie most of the way. We stop and sip from a thermos of coffee when we reach the border and watch at a roadside stop as an "iron horse" makes a long scribbly line of railroad cars move along the horizon.

A nineteenth century caterpillar, it looks like. I tell Lorry, "No wonder the Comanche and Kiowa feared that thing steaming across the open prairie as if it owned it. There's nothing out here but sky and earth and then comes the iron horse to scare the ghosts of the past.

Mouse is looking sick and showing her years. White-faced, she looks older than she is, but, like the iron horse, still chugging.

I wonder for how long though. Dogs are heaven sent and heaven delivered in so short a number of years. We have buried four Great Danes in the past ten years, plus a mongrel collie, another dachshund, a cat named Harry and a Siamese named Moonie, plus another named Kitkat. It's too much to bear.

But, in point of fact, we also have an urn in the back of the truck which contains Granpa Roy's remains. He is to be buried next to his wife in Tesuque, if we can only get there. In the powerfully devastating heat of the Texas plains, we began to think we were in a Conestoga wagon with a fading Mouse and a grawking parrot. By the way, Sam Shepherd was right when he said, "Never have a parrot."

Valle de Suerte
Tesuque, New Mexico (2016)

How does it feel to come back to the place where you built an adobe house in 1977?

Where you raised your children, where your beginnings as a writer gained ground and where you felt yourself flower as fully as you would feel in a lifetime?

I wondered if the adobe house we built -- or I should say, my cousin the builder built, and we assisted, was still the way we left it. I could feel the heavy adobe bricks made from mud and sand on our property. Each one weighed 40 pounds. There was the day we put the rustic roof beams in place, each one weighing over two hundred pounds.

I was on a ladder raising up a beam twenty feet long – my cousin on one end and me on the other, both of us on separate ladders. That was when I blacked out. When I woke, a few seconds later, my arms were locked in the same straight up position, and the beam was almost magically in place. I asked my cousin what happened. "That's what I'd like to know," he said.

I wondered if the hill-carved, two-story adobe house that wasn't our home anymore was calling for us to return

Or was it just the high dry desert call of a coyote or the dark cough of a bear?

In our return we stayed in our cousin's top-of-the-shop apartment where we could see the deer bed down under the piñon trees. Where a mountain lion brought down an antelope. Where a badger chittered angry white teeth and scared me when I took a midnight piss under a juniper tree, feeling more naked and threatened than I'd ever felt in my life.

We stayed in the top-of-the-shop where George was frightened by a frantic mouse that crawled into his cage to eat his sunflower seeds and where George, flapping crazily, broke his wing trying to escape. The next day the vet said, "Yep, his wing's broke, nothing you can do but give him tender kindness. This bird will never fly again, but the wing broke in such a way that he'll get use of it again. Just won't be able to fly, you understand"

And then there was Mouse.

Mouse, the dog.

Mouse had reached her destiny, as they say. She was tired and old and the long trip by truck across country had worn her down and one morning the little Mouse passed into the next experience and we buried her on a hillock of copper-colored sand surrounded by juniper crosses and love.

The strangeness of coming home was feeling stranger by the day.

And night. Late one night a large black bear crossed out path under the stars. It woofed a warning. Then a cough, husky and hoarse, and deep. A warning. The badger was one thing, the bear was another.

Joogii came to see us and told the Navajo bear story. Bear was a bit of a misfit. He had lost the race of the night animals and the day animals by wearing his moccasins on the wrong feet.

Joogii drew a picture of it so we could see how one foot went east and the other foot went west. That meant that bear would always be going two ways at the same time; it also meant he was a night animal and a day animal.

"But if you understand Bear," Joogii explained. "If you know about his mixed-up feet that have five toes just like a human being, then you can benefit from his healing ways, because, trust me, he has them. He has powers."

One night I hear Bear woofing under our window and I asked myself, "What is he saying?"

We had buried Mouse in the right way. Joogii had recited Navajo poems of peace and harmony: hozonhii. He had blessed the top-of-the-shop, which he called "Sky House". We had placed prayer feathers, given by George, on Mouse's grave.

Was there something I had forgotten to do?

Our lives were in disharmony. But why?

All we had done was come back to the place we loved.

Then I realized. There was one more burial I needed to attend to.

Almost thirty years had passed since we, Lorry and I, placed her mother's ashes under a two hundred-year-old juniper tree that had a dark green bed of moss under it. We scattered her ashes under this tree and then over the tears added a small vial of ash from Mount St Helens in Oregon.

Amazingly, the ash turned the moss into a rainbow of colors.

To us, it symbolized the open arms of Lorry's mother reaching out into the universe to embrace the Navajo rainbow of peace.

There was one last ceremony we had to do. And I realized it when I heard the bear cough under our window. This cough was telling us we now needed to place Lorry's mother and father together on the same bed of sacred moss.

He died when we lived in Florida and his ashes were in an urn we'd kept all these years, waiting for the time and place.

The same night we heard the bear cough, I got the urn and we carried it under the glittering stars to the arroyo and then walked in the shimmer light of the moon to the very place where thirty years before we'd spread Mom's ashes, and then later, the vibrant colored medicine ash from Mount St Helens.

As we knelt in the moonlight I heard Bear cough four times in the wind-riffled dwarf oaks.

He was near. Very near. Watching.

The last thing Dad had said was, "Tell my wife I made it to the mountain." He died shortly after that. But now we spread the thin moonlit ash from the urn on the moss under the tree and the clouds came away from the moon, and the moss place brightened. We scattered the fine soft silt of Dad's hard old life bones and they merged on the carpet of blue, white, gold, green, pink and black.

They were together at last. They both had made it to the mountain.

The following morning we returned to the burial place.

There was a bear print pointing to the juniper tree.

Acknowledgment

Some of the memories in this book previously appeared in the following publications:

Gulfshore Life Magazine
Stay Thirsty Magazine
Pearson Educational Publishing
Measured Progress
The Dragon Superpack
The Bloomsbury Review
Light Of Consciousness
Crab Creek Review
Copper Canyon Press
Silver City Review
Mind, Body Spirit

About the Author

Gerald Hausman is an award-winning, bestselling author and a regular contributor to *Stay Thirsty Magazine*. He is nationally known as a storyteller, and his books have received high praise and awards in the categories of Native America, Mythology and West Indian culture.